WRITERS on Their UNSHAKABLE
LOVE for NEW YORK

EDITED BY SARI BOTTON

NEVER CAN SAY
GOODBYE

A TOUCHSTONE BOOK
PUBLISHED BY SIMON & SCHUSTER
NEW YORK   LONDON   TORONTO   SYDNEY   NEW DELHI

Touchstone
A Division of Simon & Schuster, Inc.
1230 Avenue of the Americas
New York, NY 10020

First Touchstone trade paperback edition October 2014

For information about special discounts for bulk purchases, please contact Simon & Schuster Special Sales at 1-866-506-1949 or business@simonandschuster.com.

The Simon & Schuster Speakers Bureau can bring authors to your live event. For more information or to book an event, contact the Simon & Schuster Speakers Bureau at 1-866-248-3049 or visit our website at www.simonspeakers.com.

"The Muse of the Coyote Ugly Saloon" appears with permission from the author, Elizabeth Gilbert. It originally appeared in the March 1997 issue of *GQ* and was later the basis for the motion picture *Coyote Ugly*.

"Royalty" appears with permission from the author, Susan Orlean. It originally appeared in the September 1990 issue of the *New Yorker*.

Interior design by Akasha Archer
Interior illustrations © Shutterstock
About the cover: The front cover illustration was drawn by artist James Gulliver Hancock (jamesgulliverhancock.com), whose distinctive work has been exhibited in galleries worldwide. His book, *All the Buildings in New York*, features drawings of iconic and everyday buildings in New York, from the Flatiron and Rockefeller Center to the brownstones of Brooklyn. He lives and works in both Sydney and New York.
Cover design by Marlyn Dantes

Manufactured in the United States of America

1 3 5 7 9 10 8 6 4 2

Library of Congress Cataloging-in-Publication Data

Never can say goodbye : writers on their unshakable love for New York / edited by Sari Botton.—First Touchstone trade paperback edition.
pages cm
1. American literature—New York (State)—New York. 2. City and town life—New York (State)—New York—Literary collections. 3. Authors, American—Homes and haunts—New York (State)—New York. 4. New York (N.Y.)—Literary collections. 5. New York (N.Y.)—Biography. I. Botton, Sari, 1965- editor. II. Title: Writers on their unshakable love for New York.
PS549.N5N38 2014
810.8'03587471—dc23   2014021591

ISBN 978-1-4767-8440-3
ISBN 978-1-4767-8443-4 (ebook)

For Maggie Estep (1963–2014), a fearless great talent,
an inspiration, a badass—and a testament to the possibility
of remaining a true New Yorker long after you've left.

CONTENTS

INTRODUCTION

I'd like to begin by making one thing indisputably clear: I love New York City. I am so crazy in love with it, so excited on the occasions when I get to return to it from my home upstate, even just for brief work-related appointments on frigid winter afternoons, that I almost can't see straight.

I wanted to get that out of the way because there's been a bit of confusion about my stance on the city. To some degree, I've put together this collection of essays by some of my favorite authors about their love for New York City to clear up that confusion.

Here's the backstory. In 2013, I edited *Goodbye to All That: Writers on Loving and Leaving New York*, an anthology of essays by twenty-eight women writers, all paying homage to Joan Didion's iconic 1967 essay about quitting the city at twenty-eight. The book was published that October, which turned out to be an interesting time for it to appear.

To begin with, billionaire mayor Michael Bloomberg's twelve-year tenure was coming to a close, capping more than a decade in which the quality of life in New York City was on the upswing, as was the cost of living there. The city was cleaner and safer than ever before, making it an even greater draw for those at the higher end of the economic spectrum. Over the course of Bloomberg's three terms in office, real estate prices soared at record rates. According to a recent report by the New York City comptroller's office, since 2000, median rents have risen 75 percent while median incomes have decreased by 5 percent. That's made it unaffordable for many to stay, especially those struggling to make it in creative fields (myself included). Not to mention artist-friendly shops, bars, and restaurants. For the past several years, just about every morning I've been greeted by an outraged post or two in my Facebook feed about one haunt or another having to shut its doors, being replaced by a Chase, a Starbucks, a Duane Reade, often on the ground floor of a new, gleaming glass tower. CBGB's, Life Café, Mars Bar, Milady's Pub, Roseland Ballroom, Pearl Paint, Bereket . . . the list goes on.

Calling attention to this—and doing so just one day before my book's pub date—was an op-ed published in the *Guardian* by iconic New Yorker David Byrne (best known as a member of the rock band Talking Heads but also a painter, photographer, and author) warning that if the city became so unaffordable for artists that most of them left, he'd be joining them. "If the 1% stifles New York's creative talent," he wrote, "I'm out of here." He was echoing fellow musician Patti Smith, who in a 2010 Q&A at Cooper Union told author Jonathan Lethem, "New York has closed itself off to the young and the struggling. . . . New York City has been taken away from you. So my advice is: Find a new city." She recommended a few, including Detroit and Poughkeepsie.

Shortly after Byrne's op-ed was published, blogger Andrew Sullivan announced that after a bit more than a year of living in New York, he'd be returning to Washington. "I loved New York City with a passion until I tried to live here," he wrote in a blog post accompanied by a video of Kermit the Frog singing LCD Soundsystem's 2007 song "New York I Love You, But You're Bringing Me Down." (Sample lyric: "Your mild billionaire mayor's now convinced he's a king . . .")

Byrne's and Sullivan's declarations struck a nerve, and so did the book, which became an instant hit. Many identified with either the impetus or the need to leave New York. Some others, though, felt affronted, as if Byrne, Sullivan, and the twenty-eight authors in my book had issued a joint proclamation that the city they loved was *over* and ordered a mass exodus.

In the case of *Goodbye to All That*, nothing could have been further from the truth. But there were some people who hadn't picked up the book, who assumed, because of the title, that it contained twenty-eight anti-city screeds. They didn't know that it was (with the exception of a few essays) more like a collection of love letters to New York City, including one from me.

They didn't know that I intended for the book to be about what it *means* to people to leave the most exciting but also most challenging city in the world—the *idea* of leaving it, which I believe every New Yorker considers at one difficult moment or another, or when tempting opportunities arise elsewhere. Which is why I included essays by several women who had either returned to New York after leaving for a while—as Didion ultimately did—or who'd decided in the end that it was better not to leave at all. I even included one by an author who's never lived there—Roxane Gay—who decided that, despite a childhood fascination with the city, she was meant to love it from a distance, as an occasional visitor.

Although the people who assumed I was dissing the city seemed to be very much in the minority, I was troubled by the idea that anyone might have gotten that impression, because I am besotted with New York and always have been.

When I was a college junior in Albany, New York's state capital, I took an internship writing for the *I Love NY* campaign because I thought it would offer me the opportunity (and bus fare) to make frequent trips down to the city. I was eager to discover more of the place I'd been completely enthralled with since my early teen years and was ecstatic over the chance to write about it.

To my twenty-year-old mind, the New York that the campaign referred to *was* "the city," and I wanted a legitimate reason to spend as much time there as I could instead of being stuck three hours north in depressed "Small-bany" or on homogenous suburban Long Island, where I grew up.

Of course, the *I Love NY* campaign existed to broaden pea-brained perceptions like mine, and to extend the cool New York brand to attractions elsewhere in the far-flung state. The Adirondack Museum; the high peaks of the Catskills (technically not mountains, I would learn, but rather dissected plateaus); the Colonial saltbox houses of East Hampton; the Revolutionary and Civil War sites in Elmira—those were the kinds of tourism destinations I was assigned to visit and write about, without ever once receiving a free ride down to the city.

The internship did in fact expand my ideas about New York. I came to know a great deal about the state and its various regions and even fell in love with a few of them. But never anywhere near as deeply in love as I was—and remain—with New York City.

I longed to live there someday, and eventually I did, first in the late eighties and then again from the early nineties to the mid-aughts. It wasn't all wonderful all the time. Far from it. I lived in decrepit mouse- and roach-infested apartments with crumbling walls and noisy neighbors. I had to work long hours just to stay afloat. I had the hardest time finding anyone to date but noncommittal men who seemed to be biding their time until the city delivered on its apparent promise of a supermodel or ballerina girlfriend. In the heat of the summer I felt landlocked. In the dreary winters my mood often mirrored the dark gray slush encrusting the pavement.

But all that was just the price of admission to a city where there were more varieties of everything than anywhere else; where around every corner was a unique view, a new friend, an old friend you hadn't seen in forever; where anything was possible.

For most of the time I lived there, I was relatively certain that for better or worse, I'd never leave, even in low moments when staying felt like a marriage of convenience, the positives just barely outweighing the negatives. But then the equation shifted, and it began to seem as if, consistently, the city demanded more from me than it offered in return. It was at just that time that my husband and I got booted from the cavernous way-below-market-value East Village loft we lived in. We were priced out of the market for even most studio apartments, and so, with a bitter taste in our mouths after an expensive year in housing court, we moved upstate.

I was cranky and fed up when we left nearly a decade ago. And when I lived there, I had my issues with the city, its many demands and contradictions, as I believe most New Yorkers do. There was a piece of me outwardly copping a jaded "good riddance" pose when I said goodbye to all that. But it was little more than a thinly veiled defense, meant to mask how heartbroken I was about having no real financial choice but to leave.

I continue to have my issues with the city. Like many of the authors in this collection, I lament the rapid succession of favorite haunts shuttering. It's annoying—and frankly, mortifying—to travel in excitedly on the Trailways from upstate and make plans to meet a friend at old standbys like the Pink Pony and Max Fish on Ludlow Street, only to have the friend say, "Seriously? Both of those places have been closed for two years."

Of course, that doesn't stop me from making the trip down again and again. I'm thrilled to go and discover new haunts, and just to be there. When it's time to return to Port Authority to catch the bus home, I don't want to go. To quote that LCD Soundsystem song, warts and all, New York City is "still the one pool where I'd happily drown."

I explained this often when pressed by interviewers after *Goodbye to All That* was published. Another thing I was asked frequently was why the book included only women writers. Why no men? It's a long story, but before I even had a chance to tell it, some interviewers suggested that maybe only women write those kinds of essays. "No," I'd always respond, "that's hardly the case." In fact, some of my favorite essays about New York City have been written by men—Luc Sante's "My Lost City," Colson Whitehead's *The Colossus of New York*, E. B. White's 1948 classic "Here Is New York."

Since I first read it in college, White's meditation has always held resonance for me. It is at once timeless in its observations about the city's appeal despite all those many demands and contradictions; dated (he laments that the subway fare has risen to ten cents and refers to someone singing on the street as a "cheerful Negro"); and eerily prescient ("A single flight of planes no bigger than a wedge of geese can quickly end this island fantasy, burn the towers, crumble the bridges, turn the underground passages into lethal chambers, cremate the millions").

After mentioning "Here Is New York" in many interviews, I found myself reading and rereading it. And then it occurred to me: I could put together a collection of essays by men *and* women, inspired by White, that, unambiguously, were more about *loving* the city than about ditching it.

Here, I've wrangled some of my favorite writers into contributing essays about how they became permanently, irreversibly cemented to the place—their experiences of becoming and remaining New Yorkers, feeling as if they belong there, regardless of where they are in the world at any given time.

Just about every aspect of working on this book and its predecessor has been sheer joy for me—reading and editing authors I admire on the topic of a place I adore and long for, not to mention having cause to visit the city more often. (The bonus, as the guy named Wade in Jon-Jon Goulian's essay might say? It would be difficult for anyone to mistake me for a hater now.)

When an acquaintance learned I was working on a follow-up anthology, he asked, "What are you, some kind of representative of the New York City marketing and tourism board?" And it dawned on me that perhaps I've finally, thirty years later, created an extension to my *I Love NY* campaign internship that's more to my liking—the city edition.

Sari Botton
Kingston, New York
2014

NEW YORK, IN THE MIRROR

Rosanne Cash

I knew that New York City was my spiritual home from the age of twelve. I felt territorial from the first moment I glimpsed the city. This place knew who I was without me having to explain myself. I felt as if I'd been struggling to speak a foreign language my whole life and unexpectedly found myself dropped into the country of my native tongue.

When I was fourteen, my dad, who had a lifelong love affair with the city and kept an apartment on Central Park South for years, took me to a bespoke leather goods store in Greenwich Village called the Stitching Horse, near the famous clubs and cafés where the great folk musicians had made their marks in the 1960s. He was very familiar with the Village because of his friendships with so many of those musicians and his immersion in that scene. He had a green suede jacket made for me at the Stitching Horse. I tried it on in front of the long mirror in the store, with the light pouring in the windows from busy Bleecker Street, and everything suddenly clicked. That was my real self there in the mirror, dressed in vivid green hand-stitched suede. I belonged here. It was more than an idea; it was a sharp ache and a calling. It tugged at me for the next twenty-three years, until I pulled my entire life apart to come home.

My trips to the city increased exponentially over those years between fourteen and thirty-seven. I knew I belonged, but I didn't know how to sink roots. In the eighties, when I lived in Nashville, there was a short-lived and dodgy airline called People's Express, which flew to LaGuardia for ridiculously cheap fares. I used it like a bus, going back and forth to the city, just to feel my real self walking the streets, going to the clubs and restaurants and museums, wearing the clothes I felt most comfortable in without being whispered about, and thinking. I liked to think about my life in public, with people around me and madness just on the periphery. There was clarity inside when there was chaos outside. I once heard someone say, "We always thought she was kind of strange, but it turns out she's just a New Yorker." That was me.

I finally moved to New York in 1991. I had been living in Nashville for nine years, after growing up in California, and after spending enough time in Europe to toy with the idea of becoming a permanent expatriate in my early twenties. In Nashville I became very successful, with a string of number-one hits and a couple of gold records, but I was frustrated and felt I was not writing the songs or making the records I really wanted to make. In 1990, I wrote and produced an album called *Interiors*, which I thought was the best work of my life, and which my record label utterly rejected. At the same time, my marriage was falling apart. I was despondent. Only one thing made sense. New York.

My first apartment was at 13 Morton Street, on the corner of Morton and Seventh Avenue, a block west from the famous Matt Umanov Guitars on Bleecker Street and a block east from the original Shopsin's on Bedford Street, the gritty diner run by outrageously foul-mouthed and bad-tempered Kenny Shopsin, who had nine-hundred-plus items on the menu. (My favorite memory: Me: "I'll have French fries." Wait-ress, who was also Kenny's wife, slamming her pencil into her order pad: "Don't piss him off.")

I painted my apartment lavender and paid a year in advance. There was a tiny realtor's office on the ground floor, and the woman who worked there, Velvet, helped me carry the stroller containing my two-year-old daughter, Carrie, up the stoop and into the building every time she saw me.

The first song I wrote while living on Morton Street was the lyrics to "Seventh Avenue." I gave them to John Leventhal and he wrote a mel-ancholy melody. That was the beginning of my New York songwriting, my collaboration with John, and the seed that planted a love affair that began the next year. We married in 1995.

There was a deli around the corner on Carmine Street called Jack and Jill, and they delivered a cappuccino and a muffin to me every morning. One of the few times I actually went inside the deli, a junkie bumped up against me and took my wallet. I was shocked but oddly relieved. I'd been living in New York less than a year. I was glad to get that particular initiation over with, as I knew there were more to come. It wasn't the last time it happened—I had my wallet lifted from my handbag on the M1 bus not that long ago—but it was the initial skin-thickening crime imprimatur that every new city dweller needs.

The next year, I moved to 231 Mercer Street in SoHo, just around the corner from Fanelli's, a fantastic dark little cave of a family-owned restaurant, one of the oldest in the city. While I was walking on Prince Street one day, a ranting homeless person threw a pebble and hit me in the back of the head. That was the second skin-thickener and it sealed the deal. It was the last time I took anything personally out on the streets. After that, if a construction guy made a lewd comment when I walked by, I stopped and looked him in the eye and said, "Do you have a mother? Do you have a sister?" By the time, years later, that a couple of drunk yahoos in a truck cursed me out, vociferously and profanely, for causing them to wait four seconds while I got out of a taxi, I could look at them calmly and say, almost with compassion, "You two are going straight to hell."

I had rules for myself about my New Yorker-ness. I had to show the city I respected it and that I cared enough to learn about it.

Washington Square had been a cemetery for yellow fever victims in the early part of the nineteenth century, when Greenwich Village was still a village, separate from the city, and when Minetta Creek, now Minetta Lane, still ran through the area. In the late part of the century, when Henry James was writing *Washington Square*, carriages careening through the park on muddy days dug up those old coffins. There are still twenty thousand people buried in Washington Square, a fact probably not underscored in the NYU admissions brochure, but one which gives me a little secret thrill when I walk through the park.

I admired Jane Jacobs, urban activist in the early part of the twentieth century, who successfully blocked the proposed Lower Manhattan Expressway, which would have passed directly through Washington Square Park and displaced the twenty thousand poor souls. Unfortunately, she was not able to prevent the extension of Seventh Avenue (which at the time ended at Eleventh Street and Greenwich Avenue) into Varick Street, and the razing of old buildings and churches. The extension came to be known as "the Cut," because the buildings left standing at the margins of the extension were sheared at odd angles. I used to wander Seventh Avenue near my little Morton Street apartment and pick out the buildings that had been cut and imagine how they once looked.

I went to the map room at the New York Public Library (on land that was once a reservoir that supplied water for the city) and found the earliest maps to include the streets on which I lived. There had been a brothel at the end of my block in Chelsea in the nineteenth century, just four blocks from where Walt Whitman lived while working on the docks, and two blocks from where Clement Clarke Moore, the author of "The Night Before Christmas," had a mansion and extensive grounds sloping to the Hudson River, which was a few blocks from where Edith Wharton was born, at 14 West Twenty-Third Street.

Knowing these things gave me a growing sense of territoriality, but it took me about a decade in New York to know that living elsewhere was no longer even a tiny option in the farthest corner of the smallest part of my mind. I wasn't *fit* to live anywhere else.

I had left Morton Street and moved to SoHo in 1992, but it became increasingly unpleasant during its transition to a luxury-store theme park, and I moved back to the West Village in 1993, to 241 West Eleventh Street. My kids were enrolled at Saint Luke's, on Hudson and Grove, and could walk to and from school every day. John taught five-year-old Carrie to ride her bike at the empty Bleecker Playground at Bleecker and Bank Streets on late afternoons in the spring. (By the time we bought a brownstone in Chelsea in 1996, the year after we were married, Bleecker Playground was a buzzing toddler hot spot. By the time our son Jake was born in 1999, the playground was so crowded that you could hardly find a spot of sand in which to park your baby with a shovel. By 2002, mothers were complaining to the community board that rats roamed the playground at night because of the snacks left by the children in the day, and I reluctantly switched playground allegiance closer to home, to the Clement Clarke Moore park on Tenth Ave. and Twenty-Second Street, informally known to all as Seal Park. I had a backup play area in the gardens of the General Theological Seminary on Ninth Avenue. At that point, the *Sex and the City* bus tours co-opted Bleecker Playground and it became untenable anyway.)

Chelsea had a few stores and galleries when we moved there, but it was still the province of the Chelsea Boys, and a forty-something straight woman was invisible on those streets. I liked that. The two elderly gentlemen who were perhaps the original gay couple of Chelsea lived on my block, and I befriended them. I learned that they had bought their brownstone in the early 1960s for around $25,000. I went to Saint Peter's Church on West Twenty-First Street to hear one of them play the organ. I gleaned gardening tips and commiserated with them on the death of the decades-old English ivy on the back wall behind our communal gardens, a near-tragic event. I wrote a song about them called "Jim and George." The couple next door, Phil and Chantal, became our close friends, and Chantal and I started climbing over the back garden wall between our houses in the mornings, wearing our nightgowns, to have tea together. Our husbands eventually built stairs on either side of the wall to make it easier for us to clamber, sleepy and half-dressed.

Then things started to change. Scores of galleries, fancy shops, and upscale restaurants opened. The High Line was created and masses of tourists descended on Chelsea. Multimillion-dollar condos were built overlooking the seminary gardens, and the formerly deserted little playground was locked. A hotel replaced the Desmond Tutu Center on Tenth Avenue. Google moved onto Eighth Avenue, and an ultra-upscale private school was built near the High Line.

I started to become the Disgruntled New Yorker.

We all miss what used to be, and we all feel superior because we remember it, until the third time around. The great Italian food store Balducci's moved from its original location at Sixth Avenue and Ninth Street into an imposing old bank building at Eighth Avenue and Fourteenth Street. I was thrilled, as the new location was closer to me. I shopped there almost daily. I used to run into Elvis Costello in the cheese section. Then Balducci's closed and a carpet store moved in. I bought a rug there. Or was the carpet store there before Balducci's and after the bank? I don't remember now. In a few years it will be something else, something that will be co-opted by the young people who work at Google up the avenue and live in the expensive new condos, which used to be office buildings and warehouses, and which gave Chelsea the gritty feel that it hasn't had since 2002. Big Cup coffee shop on Eighth Avenue and Twenty-Second Street, which was ground zero for the Chelsea Boys, and which handed out free ice during the blackout of August 2003, became a Thai restaurant. The fabulous Mexican restaurant Kitchen became a Mexican-food chain.

Dozens of nail salons opened.

The great old Waverly Inn on Bank Street, a funky, century-old restaurant with a greenhouse in the back where John and I had a family breakfast the day after our wedding in 1995, was bought by Graydon Carter and became the trendiest restaurant in the city.

(And sometimes things come back around, full circle. The original, beloved Barneys at Seventh Avenue and Seventeenth Street became the Rubin Museum of Art and a Loehmann's for seventeen years, but the Loehmann's part is about to become Barneys again.)

A fter the third changeover, you become more ecumenical and tolerant. It's too bad, but it's the way it is. Something *good* may replace something good, and we're not Paris, where you can dine in the same eighteenth-century restaurant and sit at the same table as Robespierre. We're still learning to value tradition.

But it's not just the favorite restaurant you lose. Thankfully, the arrogant sense of ownership also begins to erode. I used to be the person who had to be the fastest walker on the block. Now the fastest walkers are the Millennials with their fancy handbags and their pinpoint glares. Be my guest, dear Millennial, pass me by. It's a developmental phase. I used to be the person who had to stand halfway into the street so I could be the first one to get across at the nanosecond the light changed, but now I stand on the curb. I know someone who got hit by a bus. I generally give change to homeless people, and reciprocally, a homeless person once offered me a quarter when he saw that I was distractedly trying to use a pay phone with a British fifty-cent piece, after a recent trip to the UK. I took it and thanked him. Brief and important relationships develop in unlikely places, like pay phones, which were themselves important. They were the only phones that worked on 9/11.

I know one of the secrets the rest of the country hasn't figured out yet: it's not New Yorkers who are rude, it's the tourists who've seen a movie about rude New Yorkers and think they have to act the same way when they come to New York who are rude. (One of my favorite Nice New Yorker stories: I was in Bergdorf's shopping with my fellow fence-climbing friend Chantal when I noticed it was 12:55 p.m. and I was due at my shrink on the Upper West Side at 1 p.m. I asked a saleswoman if I might use a large, comfortable dressing room for fifty minutes to make a phone call. Without hesitating, she said, "Of course! Take the key to lock yourself in so no one will bother you." Her quick response made me wonder if other women had, in fact, called their therapists from a Bergdorf's dressing room. I confess that I kept trying on clothes during the session.)

I crave the knowledge of the old New Yorkers, the eighty- and ninety-year-olds who have been here their whole lives. I know a few. I know a woman who took the subway to the Pierre to get married during the record-breaking blizzard of 1947, carrying her wedding dress in a bag. There was no other way for her to get to her wedding in twenty-six inches of snow. She said she stared out the window of the train, thinking of Princess Elizabeth's wedding to Prince Philip just a month before, with the processionals and the crowds and the pomp, and laughed at the contrast. I like to imagine her in the train, holding her dress, on the way to her future, stepping out into a New York I can only dream of.

Even so, I gave birth to a bit of Old New York.

My son Jake is a rare breed: a fifth-generation New Yorker on John's side. Jake's great-great-grandparents moved to the Lower East Side from Russia. His great-grandfather, Ramon Xiques, owned a billiard saloon at number 95 Bleecker Street, a few blocks from where I got my green suede jacket, which was a few blocks from where Carrie learned to ride her bike. Great-grandfather Ramon was implicated, and eventually exonerated, in the murder of a Cuban cigar maker in his saloon. The *New York Times* wrote all about it, on January 2, 1885.

I took Jake to Montana when he was six, thinking he would enjoy the open spaces, the mountains, and rafting on the Yellowstone River. He was very quiet during the trip, and when we returned, as we exited the Holland Tunnel into Manhattan from Newark Airport, he let out a big sigh of relief. "I am so happy to see tall buildings and people I don't know," he said. "New York's the town for me, Mom." I laughed, but tears of recognition and solidarity came to my eyes.

If I long to time-travel to the New York City of the distant past, to the weddings in the blizzard of '47, to the Bowery billiard saloons and the homes of the great writers, do the recently arrived young New Yorkers dream of my New York?

I asked one—a twenty-three-year-old who works at my record label.

"Do people your age ever wonder about my New York? Or the New York of the generation before me, and the one before that? It's different than the one you know."

"We wonder how you ever found each other without cell phones," he said.

That's not what I meant.

Do you know who E. B. White and Jimmy Breslin are? Do you know the old Arts and Letters clubs of New York and who founded them? Do you know who designed Central Park? Do you know where Five Points is? (Not the restaurant. The place.) Do you know who Stuyvesant Town is named after? Have you been to Ratner's or Katz's deli on Christmas Day? Did anyone tell you that Tompkins Square Park used to be a war zone and the area around it, Avenues A, B, and C, was called Alphabet City? Did you know that Saint Luke's on Hudson Street burned to the ground in the eighties and that the hat was passed in the street to collect enough money to rebuild it while the fire was still blazing?

Did you know that there used to be taxis called Checker cabs that were bigger and more comfortable than the regular yellow taxis, and that we would sometimes let streams of regular taxis go by just to get a Checker? There used to be a club I really loved on Varick Street called Heartbreak and they played Motown every Thursday night and I went and danced by myself, with abandon. You would have loved it. There was a restaurant farther south on Varick Street called Nosmo King. This was when smoking in restaurants was still legal, and it was an early adopter of the antismoking law. It was Nosmo King. I went there a lot.

The meatpacking district wasn't always the bastion of the chicest stores, restaurants, and nightclubs. It had *one* club called Hell and *one* restaurant, Florent. Florent was legendary. It was the coolest place in the world. It didn't advertise or preen. You had to find it.

Did you know that Jefferson Library on Sixth Avenue used to be a women's prison, and that the word *catcall* came from the women who leaned out the windows to call down to the street?

If you love Bergdorf's, do you also know about Bonwit Teller, which was just down Fifth Avenue, which rivaled Bergdorf's in chic and is still mourned by those who wandered the aisles, myself included? I know people who scavenge flea markets to find the precious old purple-and-white Bonwit Teller bags and hatboxes.

Have you pored over photos of the old Penn Station and felt tears come to your eyes thinking of its destruction?

Could you ever leave this city if you knew all that, and you realized it was just a fraction of the secrets, and that your lifetime is not long enough to learn them all? The thrill of that shared knowledge, the swell of pride, and the sense of community with those who also know have become part of the rhythm of my bloodstream.

There are those who come to New York to try it on, to burn fast and furious in the workforce, deplete their need for the city and the city's need for them, and move on. And there are those who (to paraphrase the poet Rumi) have New York in them all along. I am one of those; I see New York in the mirror, and New York looks back at me.

Matt Umanov is in the same location on Bleecker, just around the corner from 13 Morton Street, and he is a friend. I got one of my best guitars from him.

Shopsin's moved to Essex Street and is apparently a lot cleaner.

The Heartbreak club is long gone, but at a parents' meeting at Jake's school recently, a dad came up to me and said he had seen me coming out of Max's Kansas City, the quintessential musicians', artists', and poets' club, in the early eighties. God, I was proud. You never know who the keepers of your memories are.

I'm married for life and don't need any more wedding breakfasts at the Waverly Inn. But the newer iteration does make a killer mac and cheese.

I hear they might be bringing Checker cabs back.

I was a Saint Luke's mom for more than a decade, then became a Saint Luke's mother of the bride when my daughter Caitlin was married there. I sometimes go to church there at Christmas or Easter, but whether I go or not, I give them money every year, in solidarity with those who stood in the street and passed the hat while it was burning.

Carrie learned to ride her bike, graduated from Saint Luke's, went back there to teach for a short time while in college at the New School, married a native, like me, and bought an apartment in Park Slope. Someday she will ask a young person, "Do you wonder about my New York?"

I was asked to be an artist in residence at the Rubin Museum of Art and have done fourteen themed musical shows in the old Barneys building. It's helped me grow as a performer in ways I couldn't have imagined. I've never minded going to shop in the Barneys at the uptown location at all, but it will be nice to have them back in the neighborhood.

I like to walk the High Line in the snow.

I found a Bonwit Teller hatbox.

Alas, the old Penn Station is gone forever but tears come for other things, and taxis are my favorite place to cry. The drivers invariably pass me tissues through the partition without being asked. Sometimes the rides are silent, but sometimes they can be rolling confessional booths (for me or for them), micro political forums, umbrella recycling centers, a free candy store (thanks, Candy Cab!), a visit to a psychic, a honking meditation center, a one-person comedy club, or the venue for one of those brief, beautiful moments that link your past and future together gently and seamlessly.

I stepped into a taxi one day, twenty years a New Yorker, and the driver glanced at me and then sighed. "Rosanne Cash," he said quietly, as if he had been waiting a couple of decades for me to get into his taxi. "I reviewed your album *Interiors* for *Rolling Stone*." He shook his head. "It should have been the lead review."

Every moment of my life that has had a glimmer of transcendence has also had a touch of time travel, a ripple in the river that goes backward and forward. Had he been waiting for me? Did he carry the rejection of the record that gave me the courage to come to New York as a banner, as a thing of pride, until I could become the New Yorker who could reclaim and understand all the forces that led me here, without any more residual guilt over the pulling apart of the fabric of my previous lives? My heart swelled. Past and future came together, gleaming in the rearview mirror, powering the headlights. You *never* know who the keepers of your memories are.

I still have the green suede jacket from the Stitching Horse and it still fits.

That's me in the mirror. This is my city.

STAY HUNGRY

Jason Diamond

My first night in New York, after a thirty-hour bus ride from Miami, where I'd been living for nearly a year while trying unsuccessfully to figure out what to do with my life, my new roommates and I went and mixed tequila shots with whiskey drinks at Odessa Café Bar on Avenue A until they asked us to leave. We took the L train home, and my last memory of the evening before passing out on my new mattress was listening to a homeless guy with a high-pitched voice singing an a cappella version of "Stand by Me." I woke the next morning in my new apartment at the edge of Greenpoint, close to the Kosciuszko Bridge, with the rush you feel when the alcohol hasn't totally worked its way out of your system, mixed with the excitement of spending my first day in the city I'd dreamed of living in since I was a kid living in the Midwest. Too anxious to stay in bed, but still trying to fight off the hangover that was looming at my temples, I took a walk. I found a little luncheonette on Nassau Avenue that looked as if the interior and prices hadn't been updated since around 1979. There was one little old Greek lady named Bee doing all the cooking. The place was a little dirty and dingy, with one fan circulating the stale August heat. The plate of eggs and potatoes she offered me, at a cost of three dollars, satisfied me to my still possibly drunk core.

Today, Odessa's bar is closed, and the little luncheonette that fed me almost daily when I started out in New York, when my savings had dwindled close to zero because I felt the need to see everything and do everything all at once, is closed too. I recently read online that the owners still think they can make the changes necessary to reverse the failing grade they received from the health department in 2008, but everybody knows better: there are no second acts in New York restaurants.

New Yorkers are all collectors, often of things we don't necessarily want or really need. Like the man I know who stacks old issues of the *Times* dating back to the 1960s in his cramped Upper West Side apartment. He told me, "You realize just how fast life moves when you live here, so I like to keep my memories nearby." I wonder if one day the newspapers might topple and crush him, and can only imagine the *New York Post*'s over-the-top headline: "Crushing News."

Most of us aren't so extreme, but we all collect something; it's part of how you hold on to your sanity in this fast-paced city—by *holding on*. For some, it's objects that serve as reminders of a different time, of the people who have moved on to places beyond the pale like Westchester or west toward Los Angeles. For others, nothing tangible is necessary—they collect memories of particular kinds of experiences. I'm one of those. I catalog, mentally, my recollections of the places I've enjoyed eating and drinking so I can savor each meal and cocktail all over again. Those memories are my favorite New York treasures.

It's possible this habit of mine developed as a result of how difficult it is for eateries and watering holes to *not* go the way of my favorite little luncheonette on Nassau Avenue. In the ten years I've lived here, I've seen so many great places come and go—like my favorite Lower East Side bars—most of them forced to close because the rents climbed just too damn high.

When I walk past the Lower East Side spot where I used to be able to get a decent burger for a few bucks that's now a nail salon, or the East Village bar that turned into a pet store offering goods for the "haute pooch," where I would enjoy a quiet Jameson neat with a bottle of High Life while the bartender played Charles Mingus for the two of us because jazz was what they always played there since they opened in the 1950s, I think about how happy those little details made me. I try to focus on that, and all the other new great places I don't yet know about that await me, instead of succumbing to grief and the urge to kvetch.

One thing most New Yorkers collect: things to kvetch about. *Kvetch* started out as a Yiddish word, but like so much culture from just about any old country you can think of, it has become part of the New York lexicon. *Kvetching* means complaining, and complaining is really what will forever keep New York the city it is. A favorite topic to kvetch about is the way things used to be, how much cheaper things once were, and how much better. When certain haunts disappear, it's hard to resist the inclination to kvetch a little.

Like DuMont on Union in Williamsburg. It will always be my go-to favorite when it comes to nostalgia. The burger place was one of the first restaurants to pop up in the early days of the twenty-first-century Brooklyn renaissance. I'd gone there for a friend's birthday. Too poor to pay for an entire burger myself, I split one with the person sitting next to me, who told me she couldn't eat an entire burger on her own. Two weeks later, another invitation to another party at DuMont; only this one I skipped, waiting on my first big check for a freelance piece I'd written along that ladder to Professional Writer status. When the check finally came through and saved my bank account from being in the red, I marched to DuMont by myself and had the one of the most memorable meals of my life. I can recall every morsel of food, each one I chewed slowly to savor the moment.

Nearly a decade later, when I was at a point in my career where I could probably afford to eat there once or twice a week if I didn't have to worry about cholesterol, I found out that the owner of DuMont had committed suicide because of financial troubles; the restaurant was evicted from its space less than a year afterward. I'd never met the guy, but I felt like I'd lost a good friend, somebody who had provided me with a brass ring to try and grab a hold of.

Particularly kvetch-worthy: bars, like terrible lovers I can't resist, that will ultimately disappoint me by closing or, worse, filling up with the types of boring people I try my hardest to avoid. Yet no matter how many have failed me, I'm still a bar romantic, because when I find a good place to drink, I dive in headfirst, and I always hope it's the real thing. In the end I usually end up disappointed.

First there was Enid's on Manhattan Avenue in Brooklyn; that's where I used to go when I lived in Greenpoint. I don't know exactly what happened there, but we went our separate ways; I got older, its clientele looked and acted too much like better versions of how my friends and I once looked and acted. There was Mars Bar, one of the last of the East Village dives that maybe had one too many requiems written after its demise in 2011. I drank there a lot, knew the bartenders, and saw the prerequisite shit that would shock non–city dwellers for all the right reasons, like crust punks pulling switchblades, and slumming models doing coke off the dirty bar. It was like a child that kept screwing up, yet I loved it unconditionally.

I had gone to Black and White bar on East Tenth before, but it had fallen out of favor with me thanks to the NYU students, the people who could afford the neighborhood's rent, and other riffraff who started drinking there. My memories prior to that were good: my friend Caleb was the bartender and would sometimes let me DJ; I met a member of the Smashing Pumpkins there, drunkenly told him I lost my virginity to *Siamese Dream*, then said, "Just kidding," and that I had actually lost it to *Loveless* by My Bloody Valentine, the album I always thought his band had wished they'd put out. He didn't think my confusion was funny, but it was just another great night at a great bar to me.

Those were good days, but soon after that, Black and White started going downhill, so I began avoiding it until proximity forced me to bite the bullet and invite the woman I'd one day marry to meet me there for a first date. It isn't as much the place anymore as the sidewalk outside it where I first saw her standing and waiting, the pavement leading to where we sat and talked, and the booth where I knew immediately she'd one day be my wife; all of it is sacred to me. I won't go back, but I'll always have that.

There was that place in Carroll Gardens with the perfect Bloody Mary that was so crowded, it took almost two hours to get a table. But you're so satisfied with that one thing, you say to yourself, "I will drink your Bloody Marys every Sunday until the end of time, good sir," only you have one too many of them and forget what you said. A few more weeks go by, and you remember how good that drink was, so you go back, only to find out that last time you'd gone was really one of the few busy days they had, and now they're closed. Now there you are, like Cain, forced to walk the streets of Brooklyn, kvetching about how there will never be a Bloody Mary as good as that one. No single person will be able to mix tomato juice, Worcestershire sauce, horseradish, hot sauce, and vodka as perfectly as they did. No bartender will stir it correctly or put in the right amount of ice. You will die swearing that was the single greatest Bloody Mary in the history of the city, and nothing will even compare as long as the earth still spins.

I've learned to treasure every meal and every drink, because I never know what tomorrow will bring. I say that not to sound morbid but because I really have enjoyed a wonderful meal at a place one day, then come upon the same spot boarded up the next. Some days it feels like the Van Leeuwen ice cream truck is following me around the city, so I take it for granted and tell myself it will be there tomorrow; then it isn't and all I can think of is how badly I want that strawberry ice cream. I will kvetch and kvetch until I can't kvetch anymore. And even though Van Leeuwen is a pretty big brand sold in stores now, and Murray's Cheese not only expanded their shop but also opened a cheese bar one storefront over, and even if it seems like Balthazar will never stop cranking out my favorite almond croissants in all the city, I honestly never know when these places I love will suddenly stop existing, another casualty of whatever New York City circumstance, and just morph into another thing to kvetch about. Another drop in an ocean of complaints about the way things are.

Hot dogs and beer at the Shake Shack in Madison Square Park during the US Open (the only thing I look forward to in August); shaking the hand of the host at Blue Ribbon Bakery because either I go there enough that he recognizes me or he's just a friendly guy; waiting in the only line I don't mind standing in at Russ & Daughters to get my bagel (light shmear of cream cheese, sable, and onions), then sitting on the bench outside and eating it while tourists pass me by. The First Avenue coffee shop I used to sit at for hours when I had nowhere else to go. The expensive steak place on MacDougal where my then future wife took me for a birthday bone-in New York strip. I hope those places never leave me; I hope I can always eat their food.

But for all the kvetching I do about what *was*, it's what is, and what will be, that keeps me loving my life in New York. All the new bars and restaurants help keep me focused on moving forward. I have had meals and drinks all over the place, always picturing myself trying to pull off that same sort of love affair in another city where the weather might be better, the rents might be cheaper, and the rats might be nonexistent, but I can't find anything to compare.

If I need an old friend, I get a burger at Corner Bistro. If I want something familiar, I get pierogis at Veselka or a smoked meat sandwich at Mile End. If I want to take an expensive vacation, I go up to Westchester and do the big tasting menu at Blue Hill at Stone Barns. If I want to sit and watch a baseball game by myself during the dog days of summer, I go to Canal Bar in Gowanus and order the bucket of mini-beers and munch on popcorn. If I want excitement, I try my damnedest to get a table at David Chang's exquisite food laboratory, Momofuku Ko.

Hemingway wrote about Paris being a moveable feast, the kind of place that stays with you for the rest of your days once you've truly experienced it. That's what this place feels like to me. No single city truly affects a person like New York does. It's one of those undisputed truths the world over; you either hate it for your own reasons, or you can't ever shake the feeling of being there. I've been here over a decade now; I've been up in the tall buildings; I saw the lights go out on Broadway during the blackout of 2003; I rooted for the Yankees when they won the World Series even though I really don't like them; I shook the hands of two mayors whose policies made me sick; I've protested things; and I've sat on my fair share of stoops. But the way I've truly experienced New York, the way I became a New Yorker, and the way it became a part of me, was through the nights spent on bar stools by myself and at long wooden tables with a dozen other people, ordering a bunch of plates to share. I've had some of the most profound conversations of my life over shallow bowls of hummus at the tiny Hummus Place that used to be on MacDougal until the supposed ten-thousand-dollar-a-month rent forced them out of the four-hundred-square-foot space. I've felt more accomplished for finding a secret fried chicken gem than for almost anything else I've ever done. The saddest thing I've ever seen in the city was when I walked past that luncheonette in Greenpoint to see the owner, Bee, standing behind a counter, longing for the days when she was allowed to serve the customers she loved their eggs and bacon.

That's my New York; it always has been and it always will be. Restaurants and bars will come and go, but I'll always have new ones to go to, drinks to drink, and meals to eat. My cup will never be empty, and my stomach will never be full. I'll always long for the next haunt and recall the old times. I'll get excited when I find a new place serving pizza that's worth the hype, and I'll tell anybody that will listen that the best chicken salad sandwich was at this small French café off Houston that made it with tarragon and grapes, in between soft, fresh challah bread. I'll kvetch because it isn't there anymore, tell people it will never be bettered, but secretly go on wishing that it would, because that's what always keeps me going in this city: the promise that my next great meal is just around the corner.

NEW YORK AND THE NIGHT

Patricia Engel

Like most kids who grow up in New Jersey, I couldn't wait to get the fuck out. There were things I liked about the northern suburbs just a few miles from the George Washington Bridge: mountains, pumpkin patches, colonial cemeteries, the sight of foxes and deer wandering through the forest near our house, and the annual Cabbage Night ritual of vandalizing the neighborhood with toilet paper and shaving cream. Everything else, I could leave and never miss. And my parents, bored art-loving Colombians adrift in conceptually idyllic Angloville, took my brother and me to the city as often as possible: weekends at museums, the opera, wandering art fairs and Village streets, browsing bookstores and galleries. When we were teenagers, our parents encouraged us to develop our own relationships with the city: we went to rock concerts at the Roxy and Roseland, saved up to buy leather jackets and boots in the East Village, and mastered the subway. They knew suburban ennui could be enough to kill a kid and wanted us to know there was more to life than football games and the mall.

They told us the city was ours. There were no outsiders here. And maybe that's why I always had the feeling the city was waiting for me to grow up so we could finally be together and start our great affair.

When it was time, I applied to many colleges but the only one I wanted to go to was NYU and they were the first to accept me.

Thus began my decade in New York.

Almost twenty years now removed from my arrival in Manhattan, I can see that my love with the city began and intensified over a series of nights when its allure and mystery were at their highest, flaws covered by that golden sheen of darkness and ambient light.

I remember my first winter. Eighteen years old, enjoying a night out with my new friends at the now defunct Spy Bar on Prince Street, a huge living room filled with red velvet and baroque furniture under enormous chandeliers. Somewhere around three or four in the morning we decided it was time to go home and found that while we'd been in our cave, over two feet of snow had fallen. There were no taxis to be found and the streets were not yet plowed. We walked together until we had to part to go our separate ways, wading through the snow—me in my short knit dress and knee-high black leather boots, the snow slipping in through the tops and turning soupy around my calves. But the night was electric, fused with majesty in the calm that had overtaken the city, turning Washington Square Park into a pillowy heaven. I walked alone up Fifth Avenue to my dorm on Tenth Street, the only person as far as I could see in any direction. The city was *all mine*, and I loved it.

The next morning, the city was a slushy mess, and I spent it warm in my dorm with my suitemates, all Tisch acting students—from Ohio, South Jersey, and Japan—ordering in Chinese takeout and helping them rehearse lines for class. Sometimes I'd go visit the guys who lived in the next room over, one of whom rarely left his computer and would tell me about chat rooms and this really cool new thing called the World Wide Web.

The following summer, I was living with a pair of heroin addicts from Pennsylvania who'd leave their used syringes in clusters around the apartment. I'd often have to fish them out from under my brush piles and canvases for my painting class. They were saving them to bring back to the needle exchange, they told me, and I got used to being extra careful. I was somehow not even especially fazed when one, frothing at the mouth, pulled a gun on a friend for spilling nail polish remover on the kitchen counter. I'd never seen a gun so close. It was surreal to have it pointed at our faces. But I was not scared. Later, my friend and I went to the diner downstairs and over a plate of fries we took a little pride in the fact that we were getting the sort of life education we'd both craved during the years we'd each spent hibernating in suburbia.

She was one of the dozen or so friends I made my first week in New York—friends I felt I'd been waiting for all my life. We came from all over but somehow destiny placed us in all the same classes that semester and we gravitated toward each other immediately. It was only later that we realized we were all either immigrants or the children of immigrants. Every one of us. We'd all grown up with a sense of displacement that faded as soon as we arrived in the city and found each other. To this day, they remain my dearest friends.

Along with more friends, jobs, and more apartments all over town, there were many romances that took root during my New York years, most of which bloomed in the night, on park benches, apartment stoops, on long strolls home after sitting across from each other at tiny restaurant tables. My favorite of those nights also took place in winter—an unusually frigid November night when the boy, whom I'd met months earlier at a concert at Irving Plaza, and I went out to Union Square to watch a lunar eclipse. We stood leaning against one of the walls along the east side of the park, wrapped into each other for warmth of every kind, watching the shadow of the earth pass slowly in front of the moon. That night I knew I loved not only the city but the boy in my arms, because he understood my need to be enchanted, to go out under the starless sky and be amazed.

Like any flourishing New Yorker, I eventually became cynical. After a few years, I felt restless and went to Paris. When I returned a year later, the city felt both old and new to me. Rather, *I* felt old and new. I took to exploring parts of the city I'd never known, made new friends, exposing myself to new subcultures and communities. And I discovered this was the best thing about New York: you could run away every day if you wanted to and still find yourself in a newly incarnated version of the city. You never had to be the same person. You could disappear and be found all at once.

The nightlife was always my friend. I was dedicated to her with a stamina that astonishes me now. The nights were rich and plentiful at clubs and bars—places that exist now only in memory or by new ownership and going by other names. These were nights when I thought we could live on music—when most nights involved seeing a band play that the rest of the country would discover a year later, when I thought DJs had one of the noblest professions, when I thought the revelers and painted drag queens who danced with me would be at my side forever and that I would grow old with the regulars at the neighborhood bar, which we nicknamed "the Regal Beagle," our own interminable after-hours haunt. We were young. We were so sure about everything. And we were so wrong I have to smile.

My years in the city had their darkness that didn't come from just the sunset. I watched the great mushroom cloud rise over the collapsing Twin Towers from my window, and the smell that fell over Lower Manhattan for months is one I will never forget, along with the sight of the National Guard stationed at the corner, a shrine to the fallen in our park, or the night I received terrorist threats on my answering machine that brought the FBI to my front door. There was the night I watched a neighbor run bloody-faced into the hallway because her husband was trying to kill her. Or when a friend's mother disappeared while walking the family dog, her body found months later floating in the East River. And the night a friend called to tell me that another friend, a brilliant young artist, had been strangled and drowned by her own boyfriend in a bathtub.

There were the friends who became ill, with depression, addiction, HIV, cancer, and other sicknesses. There were hospitalizations and funerals and trials and suicide attempts and rehab stints. There were chance encounters that turned into love stories, engagements and weddings and babies. And sometimes there were breakups and divorces and lots of therapy. There were professional achievements to celebrate, new, better apartments to move into, and always that feeling when you walk out the door and onto the street in New York that today, no matter what happened yesterday, you can begin again.

During this decade, I was always writing. Alone, for myself, to keep entertained while cultivating another career that I found profoundly unfulfilling. I knew I wanted to be a writer but had no idea of the practical route one is supposed to take to become one, and though I knew many artists, I didn't run with an especially literary crowd. The only thing I knew to do that would help me become a better writer was to read a lot and accumulate more experiences. I put my focus into traveling, all over the world, but I always kept New York as my home base. How could I trade it for some other place, when it had been so good to me, giving me friends that were like family, giving me days and nights that expanded my heart so much I felt at times I couldn't contain the love in me?

But the very landscape of New York started to cause me discomfort. The lack of open horizon became physically disorienting. Every time I returned from a trip and stared out the window as the plane descended over the New York area, I felt my entire body tighten in repulsion. The conversations with the friends I so loved, over lunch, over drinks, over coffee, over dinner, over wine on their couches, became tiresome, and that endless trot between enclosed spaces, noise among the confinement, started to give me anxiety. I needed air that didn't smell like exhaust. I needed to walk on the street and not bump into other bodies. I needed silence without sirens and car horns. I needed to be in the walls of my own home and not smell the weed my neighbors were smoking or know what song was playing on their speakers. I needed to have my face not sting when I stepped outside in the cold.

I needed to walk through the city and not feel I was in a vault of my life's sorrows and broken dreams, with bars and restaurants and parks and particular street corners serving as landmarks for turns my life should or should not have taken, for people I once knew whom I didn't know anymore, for people I thought I would love for a very long time who did not feel the same way: pinpoints of a map of my life, places I'd been when I fell in love, told someone goodbye forever, or received very bad news.

New York started to feel like a very small town, all the faces familiar and predictable. I'd become familiar and predictable too.

I once got a tattoo on Saint Mark's Place, to commemorate some monumental period in my life I thought I'd want to remember forever. Two years later, I had the tattoo removed because I felt it bound me to a past I'd shed in every other way and no longer wanted the branding on my flesh to remind me of it every day.

I was starting to feel about New York the way I came to feel about that tattoo.

By twenty-seven, I watched the night mostly from my window, sitting on the radiator, with the growing awareness that as much as I loved New York, we just weren't right for each other anymore. We needed time apart, and because New York would never be the one to reject me, I knew I had to be the one to end things, at least for now. I'd loved New York so faithfully for so many years but I needed something else.

I thought this day would never come but here it was.

I, like many New Yorkers, couldn't wait to get the fuck out.

So I chose Miami. The excuse was graduate school, though people told me I was crazy to *leave* New York in my effort to become a writer. But I knew I needed more space and silence for both my body and my mind. It was time for a new city to seduce me, to awaken my senses just as New York had done for me that night so many years ago when I walked home alone in the snow.

Leaving wasn't easy. I wasn't only leaving the city but just about everyone I loved and who loved me. In the beginning, going back to visit was difficult too. I still felt torn between my love for New York and my fresh romance with Miami, ever sexy and soothing, and felt guilty that I was more productive in my writing in this new town than I'd ever been in New York and that's what I needed now. I felt conflicted leaving New York again at the end of every visit, but also relieved to fly back down south, the ocean and clean breeze and warm sun waiting for me.

As I write this, I'm closing in on a decade here in Miami, but I still go back to New York often. It's not the same city it was when I left, but I don't mind that because I am not the same girl, and I will never judge New York, the way New York never judged me.

My emotional ties to the city have only deepened with the distance. Whenever I'm there, I steal a few moments by myself out in the night with only the city for company and I thank it for all it gave me, for the years of rapture and for the beautiful world it put at my feet.

New York is still the place I consider home. Or at least, the place I consider *more* home than any other home I've known. And I know it will be ready to take me back and give our love another try one day when I finally return for good.

TO LIVE AND DIE IN NEW YORK

Phillip Lopate

I am a native New Yorker, which means I was ruined in the crib for life elsewhere. The milk I drank from my mother's breast probably contained window soot or was diluted with traces of Rheingold beer and egg creams. We are all familiar with E. B. White's division of New Yorkers into three categories: the one who was born here and, like myself supposedly, "takes the city for granted and accepts its size and its turbulence as natural and inevitable"; the one who commutes into work each day; and the third "who was born elsewhere and came to New York in quest of something." It is from this last group of provincial questers that most of the disillusioned literary pieces about leaving New York are drawn. I find such essays, from Fitzgerald to Cheever to Didion (not to mention a recent anthology about quitting New York), however graceful stylistically, finally tedious and beside the point. They came here for a party and overstayed; poor dears. They viewed it in their twenties as a Mecca for the young and then got older; tsk tsk! As a native New Yorker, which is to say an old soul who never believed in the glamour of youth, who has tried to live in other climes and come around to electing this city as my catafalque and final resting place, I have no choice but to embrace it with ardor. Disillusionment is not an option.

I sometimes think back with incredulous wonder to the first half of the twentieth century, when New York was regarded as the capital of modernity, the futurist city par excellence. European writers like Paul Morand, Louis-Ferdinand Céline, and Maxim Gorky would come here to gape at the frenzied, heartless, skyscraper dystopia in store for them, like some robotic set out of Lang's *Metropolis*. I am permanently denied that culture shock because for me New York is a worn and familiar old shoe—and I emphasize *old*. It seems increasingly like an elderly dowager, wearing its architectural history of cast-iron loft buildings and art deco Cathedrals of Commerce and Brooklyn brownstones and six-story tenement Bronx walk-ups and Greek revival museums and Rockefeller Center with imperturbable valetudinarian stubbornness. It has serious cracks in its infrastructure, certainly. But I could say, with Montaigne, "All that totters does not fall. The fabric of so great a body holds together by more than a single nail. It holds together even by its antiquity, like old buildings whose foundations have been worn away by age, without cement or mortar, which yet live and support themselves by their own weight."

Meanwhile, the future has moved off elsewhere.

In place of the future is that recurring trope: that New York is ripe for apocalypse. The destruction of New York by fire, Godzilla, flood, or nuclear weapon has been enacted countless times with grisly satisfaction on film, just as its demise has been predicted in forty-year cycles by pundits and social critics taking its pulse. It does not seem right to these experts that it can continue so recklessly reinventing itself, so it must be dying. But it is not. It survives, warily and agnostically, as befits a colony that was started by the Dutch not for religious reasons but simply to make money.

There is a certain muscular set in a New Yorker's face that reveals the owner's tension, exasperation, wariness, elation, and expectation in easily legible layers. Or so I find it. When I lived in Houston or San Francisco and took public transportation there, I looked at the other bus riders and could not begin to imagine what they were thinking. But I have the sense (which could be completely misguided) that I can read the faces of New Yorkers, can easily slip into their streams of consciousness. This conviction—so important for a fiction writer—has nothing to do with any special attribute of New Yorkers: it simply means that I am a local here and would probably feel the same ease of identification with the populace's inner lives if I had been a native all my life of Cairo, Illinois, say. On the other hand, maybe it does have something to do with the specific character of New York, because the greatest asset of this city is its plentiful public space. In its streets, parks, subways, even its semipublic spaces like schools, hospitals, libraries, restaurants, you feel you have the right to be there and to enjoy the company of strangers, about whom you are free to speculate. You are equally free to wallow in loneliness, self-pity, and alienation, though I myself never feel completely lonely or self-pitying if a swarm of people surrounds me. Like Whitman, I am energized by the crowd and momentarily a believer in democracy.

We are often warned that our public space and urban characteristics are threatened—a phenomenon linked to what Richard Sennett diagnosed as "the fall of public man." The civic sense gives way to the corporate: the corporation builds a tower on Park Avenue and grudgingly sets beneath it a plaza, which it polices to discourage the homeless and other "undesirables." The expanding museum takes another nibble out of Central Park. The sports complex leaves only inches between itself and the waterfront fence for walkers. Suburban-type malls with franchise stores replace mom-and-pop candy stores. And so on. But what I see happening in New York, over the long haul, is more dialectical: a forfeiture of public space here, a restoration and expansion of it there. We get the new High Line and the Brooklyn Bridge Park and the Bronx River Park, the Louis Kahn–designed FDR memorial on Roosevelt Island and the recreational plans for Governors Island; the streets are reconfigured for pedestrians and bicycles, car lanes are taken away. The habit of public space, with its clashing urban textures and mingling of social classes, is too deeply woven into New York to disappear. It is premature to mourn the loss of the soul of New York—another apocalyptic scenario, promoted by those who are tempted to quit it.

Do I seem overly optimistic? No, it is simply that I have seen this city go through so many economic declines and rebounds, so many real estate booms and busts, so many community control decentralizations followed by municipal centralizations, so many alternations of Left and Right, so many corrupt, crooked politicians of all stripes, followed by so many investigations and cleanups, that I have grown both cynically and idealistically confident that New York will somehow land on its feet.

My favorite place to be in New York is the subway. I love to sit down (if I can find a seat) and look around and see the human hand that has been dealt me. A mother and her squirming little boy to my right, a fat man sleeping across the aisle . . . Have you noticed how often people sleep in the subway? Even standing up they close their eyes, summoning dreams or just gray oblivion. Of course, you could say that they close their eyes to ward off having to take in the strangers around them, which is the misanthropic interpretation; I prefer to think they feel so comfortable in the subway that they let themselves go, maybe even more so than they might in the privacy of their homes. Some contemporary poet should update Whitman's "The Sleepers" and write a great ode to the subway passengers rocking in the rickety arms of Morpheus and the MTA.

And then there are the subway readers of difficult books. I like to imagine that New Yorkers are more literate than the riders of other American metropolises. When I was a college student, taking the subway all the way from Brooklyn to Columbia, I used to read fat Russian novels such as *The Idiot* or *Anna Karenina* with the covers conspicuously exposed, always hoping against hope that some pretty, unattached woman nearby would be impressed. And if *she* were the one reading a great classic, I would fantasize engaging her in a long conversation about what she thought of the book, whether she liked it or not, and then we would make love, get married, and have babies. I still take tomes back and forth (most recently, rereading *The Magic Mountain*) on the subway, and try to peek at the titles of my fellow riders, although now it doesn't matter whether the person beside me is a man or a woman, I simply want to know what educated young people are reading. If an attractive girl is deep into a paperback by a hip, trendy writer such as R*** M**** or D*** E*****, I am immediately disheartened. What's the use? I think. I have never spotted anyone on the subway reading one of my books (though others have reported such sightings to me). But just today I saw a nice-looking young woman take out of her purse Primo Levi's *Survival in Auschwitz* and start to read with concentration, wrinkling her nose at what must have been a horrific passage. You can't get much better than Primo Levi. Come to think of it, once I saw a couple take out matching paperbacks of Plato's *Republic*, which they were probably assigned for a class, and start to imbibe the noble Athenian's philosophy. It was almost enough to balance out all the young people playing dumb games on their cell phones.

What I like especially is when the subway rises above ground for a few stops, the way it does on the F train at Smith and Ninth Street and Fourth Avenue, and I can see the whole city spread out around me. The light is so beautiful suddenly. I remember reading a comment from Norman Mailer, decades ago, when he wrote for the *Village*

Voice, that the New York subways were a disgrace, like the Black Hole of Calcutta. First of all, I don't think Norman had ever been to Calcutta, so why was he defaming the place, and second of all, I just don't get it, this denigration of our magnificent mass transit. The subways, to my eyes, are a godsend: efficient, they get me where I want to go pretty quickly, they provide entertainment, sometimes via musicians who perform at station platforms, sometimes through the singing panhandlers who traipse through the cars, and most important, they are a stay against solipsism, proof positive that I am not alone in the universe.

It will be argued by proponents of other burgs that virtually everything I have spoken of in New York's favor can be found in other cities. I don't dispute that. New York does not have to be unique for me to love it. In truth it *is* unique, partly because of its having this particular set of desirable attributes all in one place, and partly because of its piquant mixture of beauty and ugliness, which I choose to call reality. When I am visiting other places around the world, they may strike me as lovelier, more orderly, more sensually alluring, what have you, but something is missing. I feel a thinning of the reality oxygen. When I am in New York, however, I feel up against the tragic and the sublime. The substance of life, in all its stimulating potential for grimness, grandeur, and folly, is conveyed to me by these very streets, these buildings, these surroundings. Is it simply grandiosity that fosters my identification with New York? You cannot separate me from it. The Brooklyn Bridge is my mother, the Empire State Building my father. The ichor of my blood is from the Gowanus Canal, the lymph that flows in my veins is Hudson River–drawn. My limbs and my head are the five boroughs.

Narratively speaking, there are the things that happened to New York and the things that happened to me, and the two get tangled up in my mind. Cicero said it: "Such is the power of places to call up memories. And in this city this is infinite: for wherever we walk we set our foot on history." All the city's catastrophic scars I seem to have registered, in however vestigial a manner: the Dutch massacre of the Indians, the Revolutionary War conflagration that burned down half of Manhattan during the British army's occupation, the typhus plague, the Civil War draft riots, the sinking of *General Slocum* ferry, the Triangle Shirtwaist factory fire . . . When the World Trade towers fell on September 11th, I thought my city was under attack: it took me a while to register that all of America had been assaulted. The bad mayors and the good—Jimmy Walker, LaGuardia, O'Dwyer, Impelleteri, Wagner, Lindsay, Beame, Koch, Dinkins, Giuliani, Bloomberg, De Blasio—I took them all personally. The 1929 stock market crash was both a national event and a local one: my father was nineteen when the stock market crashed, and it branded him forever. He had been a budding newspaperman, but the papers he wrote for bankrupted, and so he went to work in a factory and turned cautious, frightened to lose his job. Under his influence I grew up similarly cautious, afraid to take out car loans or second mortgages.

It works the other way as well: New York's excessive pride, chauvinism, provincialism, and superiority complex have left their special mark on me, and I have gone through life with an arrogance which is not the less irritating for being largely unconscious. I feel entitled to speak up, to have my say. That edge of self-confidence that comes from being a native son of the center of the universe, the Capital of the Twentieth Century (it remains to be seen which metropolis will claim the twenty-first), is balanced, I would hope, by the stoical resignation every New Yorker feels in the face of enormities we cannot control, of all that is outside our power. For as much as we are schooled in arrogance, we are also trained to feel powerless before the whims of Chance and Greed, the deities that run this city.

THE GOODBYE GIRL

Anna Holmes

I fell in love with New York twice. Once in 1996, while in the middle of a deep depression and living in a decaying three-story shingled building in North Brooklyn. The second time in mid-2002, almost eleven years after I first arrived, while sitting in the middle of the Brooklyn-Queens Expressway.

But let me back up a bit.

August 1991. It was sweltering and miserable inside my taxi from Newark Airport to Greenwich Village; the A/C was on the fritz and the window on the rear passenger-side door wouldn't roll down. The Pulaski Skyway was a disgusting, decrepit mess, but in the distance I could see the sun glinting off the vertical steel spines framing the corners of the World Trade Center buildings, and, to the left, the Empire State. I was eighteen years old. I had come to the city because I needed to escape. Escape from my hometown in California. From my parents. My sister. My tiny bedroom, whose walls felt like they were closing in on me. From the smug privilege and overdeveloped sense of entitlement epidemic among my peers, who took it for granted that they would always be safe, always be well-off, always be beautiful, always be, like everyone else around them save for me and a few other folks, white. And maybe, from me.

New York offered an opportunity to get an education not just in the humanities but in life: a crazy, messy, dirty, diverse, challenging, sometimes even dangerous life. I went from my tiny California bedroom to a tiny Union Square dormitory, and then a series of tiny East Village apartments. But the world—meaning New York—seemed so big and so hungry, I feared it might swallow me up. I kept to a routine: By day, I attended classes at the private university I had chosen to attend, and to which I would eventually owe over $100,000. By night, I worked in the university's computer lab, or sprawled on the floor of the rental I shared with my boyfriend, drinking beer, smoking pot, playing backgammon, having sex, and driving one another—in my case, literally—crazy.

Flash forward to June 1995. College was over, as was the relationship—my first, and, I believed after its implosion, my last. After graduation, devastated by its traumatic but necessary end and just beginning to grapple with the aftereffects of its toxic blend of codependency and emotional and substance abuse, I sought comfort in friends and a brief residency in my home state of California. I was back in the city by November. New York, it was clear, was not done with me, or I with it. By January, however, I had begun fantasizing about killing myself.

My state of mind, which up until that point had been fragile but forward-looking, took a turn for the worse during that winter of 1995–96. Maybe it was the season; maybe it was the return to reality. Maybe it was the fact that I was only twenty-two. It didn't really matter: the depression that had been building had burst forth with brutal consequences, not just for my psyche but for my very sense of place. As those who have suffered from it know all too well, major depression can make even the most fun-loving scenarios seem sinister, and the way my illness warped my experience of New York, though not particularly original or surprising, was nevertheless profoundly unsettling. The canyons of buildings up and down the avenues felt suffocating and claustrophobic, not celebratory or characteristic of the decades of human ingenuity and achievement that had brought them to bear. Trees lining the city's side streets were emblems of incarceration, not optimism. The living, breathing mass of people on the sidewalks and in the subways was no longer an expression of the city's creative and civic collaboration but a reflection of the worst and most mercenary aspects of humanity. In short, I had a bit of a case of the Travis Bickles, the suicidal ideation and mild hallucinations without the male entitlement. It was a dark, lonely, and absolutely terrifying place to be.

My therapist wasn't helping to extract me from my fugue. Neither were my friends, as much as they tried. Eventually, I decided that the only way to keep myself alive—save a trip to the nearest hospital's mental health ward—was to write. So, in February 1996, I opened a black leather notebook, grabbed a pen, and began making a list of the things I had once enjoyed about life, a reminder of the reasons I had for living. Loved ones were, of course, toward the top. Further down, I scribbled words and phrases like "birds singing," "Stevie Wonder music," "fireflies," "blackberry cobbler," and "road trips." At one point, I wrote, "Early evening light in summer."

The black notebook, or the Reasons for Living Journal, as I thought of it, was as much a talisman of why I should reject the utter despair that accompanied my depression as it was a love letter to the city of New York, which at that point I had lived in for only five years. (I would live in it for seventeen-plus years more.) Fort Tryon Park and the Cloisters went on the list, as did pastrami sandwiches from the Second Avenue Deli. Gargoyles on Financial District facades made an appearance, as did the men who played backgammon and chess in Washington Square Park. As the depression deepened and soured, the list grew longer, though sometimes all I could squeak out of my gnawed-on Bic and overwhelmed brain were lazy homages to accepted fan favorites like "baby cheeks" and "banana split sundaes."

Finally, mercifully, someone prescribed me Prozac, and the hallucinations faded away, as did my fantasy of leaping from one of the city's dozens of bridges or thousands of subway platforms. But the lessons in that journal, the mantras I had been scribbling and repeating and invoking, did not. In fact, I kept writing in it, and soon the entries became less parts of a list than elements of an ongoing collection of observations; I was remembering not only to appreciate the little things in life but to notice them in the first place. With my mental health still somewhat fragile, this required a certain recasting of the city's more distasteful elements, but more broadly, the development of a curiosity about almost everything and anything I came across. I still remember the day I realized that the city's sidewalks and subway platforms, though filthy, were also accidental public art canvases, gray slabs speckled with black wads of once-juicy and colorful chewing gum that had been discarded, darkened, and ground down into the concrete by thousands of pedestrian footfalls. For weeks after, I could look at nothing else. Then there was the discovery, later that spring, that short, sharp clicking sounds with my tongue would summon the squirrels living in and among the grassy walkways of Union Square and Stuyvesant Town, hungry for a cashew or two. (I always obliged.)

My forced inquisitiveness about the city, this privileging of possibility and patience over the impulse to hurl pell-mell through life—not to mention every subway station, park, and avenue—eventually proved effortless: an optimism that, with enough practice, became a habit and a useful corrective to my still-just-under-the-surface depression and anxiety disorders. (The continued Prozac prescriptions didn't hurt either.) In the summer of 2000, I moved to westernmost Queens—Long Island City, to be exact—and settled into a sunny studio apartment with ample outdoor space for my two young cats. Fifteen months later, in the early autumn, a passenger plane crashed into the World Trade Center. I could see the gaping, smoking, jagged maw from the end of my street, which offered an unobstructed view of downtown Manhattan. A few minutes after I ran home, hyperventilating, and turned on the TV, another aircraft had plunged into the complex. It would be the beginning of the second time I would learn to love New York.

I stayed close to home in the weeks after the attacks. Part of this was fear: fear of further violence, fear of inhaling the noxious cloud of steel and office furniture and jet fuel and human flesh that was wafting over into Brooklyn and, when the wind was right, to my studio apartment. Part of it was fascination: I could not keep my eyes off cable news; I even slept with it on, waking once every two to three hours to wrestle my glasses over my ears and take a quick glance at the headlines, which sadly (or thankfully) hadn't changed. In October, the fear overcame the fascination—I had begun to aurally hallucinate the sirens of emergency vehicles—and I began to think seriously about leaving. The skies of Long Island City were still broad and bright, and the birds still congregated in the branches of the leafy, molting oak tree in the empty lot next door, but the city felt claustrophobic again. Uncertain, unsettling, small, vulnerable. I perused online real estate listings for apartments and bungalows in Santa Barbara and Ventura Counties, even made some phone inquiries. I decided that I probably needed a car to live in California—or just in case I had to flee the city at a moment's notice—so I emptied my already meager savings account, purchased a dependable Toyota, and made tentative plans as to how and when I would make the journey across the country.

But a funny thing happened on the way to leaving New York: I ended up staying.

The impetus for my change of heart wasn't so much the city's oft-remarked-upon post-9/11 civic resilience but something entirely more selfish: the car suddenly gave me the opportunity to see and do more stuff. Fall settled in, then winter arrived, and the smells of the death pile downtown slowly faded away, and the sounds of sirens—real and imagined—retreated slowly into the background of the white noise that was the city soundtrack. I began taking my new car out for a spin once a day; at first, to determine the easiest and most efficient ways to escape the city—north on Twenty-First Street in Astoria to Hoyt Avenue, then a right, then soon another right, then another, and straight onto 278 and over the Triborough Bridge to the mainland—and later, driven by curiosity and a desire to learn as much about the city as I could before I departed, to investigate what lay beyond my little bubble on the East River. I discovered Astoria Park, where elderly women did tai chi in the shade and joggers moved swiftly under the eerily familiar fixed trusses of the Hell Gate Bridge. (I would learn that the Hell Gate, opened in 1916, served as the inspiration for the larger, more majestic Sydney Harbour Bridge.) A little bit to the east, I could park my car in the lot of an airport hotel off Astoria Boulevard and watch the planes do their deep dives upon their final approaches to LaGuardia. (A fifteen-minute drive from the airport hotel was the best Thai food I'd ever had the pleasure of eating.)

Excited and stunned by the possibilities of a city I had actually never really seen or read about—periodicals that purport to offer portrayals of city life do little but chronicle the assignations of upper-class Manhattanites—I broadened my search area to include other parts of my borough, not to mention all others. I drove to Queens landmarks and parks and beer gardens and sprawling cemeteries smack dab in the middle of industrial districts; to Italian-American specialty stores in parts of the Bronx and southern Brooklyn; to malls and miniature golf courses in suburban Staten Island; to the seaside art deco bathhouses of the Rockaway Peninsula; to the Latin-American food vendors of Red Hook, Brooklyn, and to the abandoned, weed-covered runways of Floyd Bennett Field. At one point, in January 2002, I realized that I hadn't responded to the latest follow-up from my real estate agent in Ojai, California, and that my car, which had been obtained in order to execute an escape, had provided me an abandon I hadn't experienced in a long time. It was almost as if the rejection of my adopted home had provided me a fresh set of eyes and a freedom through which to embrace it all over again. Queens, in particular, began to hold a special place in my heart: a noisy, messy congregation of skin colors and languages and income levels that, more than any strip of lily-white Upper East Side condos or historic district of Brooklyn brownstones, seemed to symbolize what New York was all about.

I remember the specific day I fell in love with the city once again, when the love affair reignited in full. It was May 2002, and I was driving back from a trip to Boston. Over the Whitestone Bridge I went, then to the Grand Central Parkway, and then to the BQE, which would take me to McGuinness Boulevard in Brooklyn, and then—whoosh—up to and over the Pulaski Bridge and back to my studio by the river. But traffic on the BQE had begun to slow down when I passed Northern Boulevard, and by the time we approached the LIE, it was inching forward at a glacial pace. The climb up the Kosciuszko Bridge was agonizing—all box delivery trucks and windowless vans and Lincoln Town Cars blaring their horns and jockeying for position—and then, up at the top, it stopped altogether. It was seven p.m., but it was almost summer and the sky was still light, still thirty minutes or so to the gloaming. I put on the parking brake, turned off the 1010 WINS traffic report, and gazed around me. To the east were the ordered gravestones of the Mount Olivet and Mount Zion cemeteries, and, further on, the lights of Shea Stadium. To the south were the headlamps of a string of LaGuardia-bound aircraft, the Williamsburgh Savings Bank clock tower and, further off, the faint twinkling of the necklace lights of the Verrazano-Narrows Bridge. To the west, I saw the steel husks of industrial Greenpoint, Brooklyn, and beyond, a tug on the East River dwarfed by the mighty Midtown Manhattan skyline. To the south, a faint glow at that terrible place in lower Manhattan where thousands of men and women were about to complete the grim task of cleanup and recovery. Early evening light in the summer, indeed. It had been a long time coming—over ten years, in fact—but I finally felt like I'd arrived. (Maybe. Sort of.)

A GUY NAMED WADE

Jon-Jon Goulian

In 1986, when I was a freshman at Columbia, I met a guy I'll call Wade who looked a touch like Henry Rollins, the same hard stare and thin angry lips, but a foot taller, and who was always spittling away about how much New York City "fuckin' sucks" and how "heavily duped" he had been to go to school there. Duped by whom I couldn't figure out. I tried to press him on that issue many times, but Wade didn't like being pressed. He had been the star of his high school in central Florida. A "triple threat," as he put it: "Good on the field, good in class, good in the sack." No one ever pressed him on anything. Even when I tried to press him gently—"Wade, I'm not understanding something. Did anyone *force* you to come here?"—he would deflect it: "Did anyone force *you*?" Which wasn't to the point, because I wasn't complaining.

When Wade got drunk, an increasingly common occurrence as our first semester wore on, reaching a perilous high of seven days a week by late November, he came close to opening up. His words would get lost in his mouth, and his face would get pretty twitchy, which made it hard to follow him, but from the bits I managed to glean, he had been duped by everyone. There was a reference to a college

counselor in high school who was a "dumbfuck." There was a reference to a Columbia "brochure," occasionally an "admissions catalog,"
that had "lied." A commercial with Ed Koch in it was somehow responsible. His parents were also to blame. "Fooled by the glamour of the
Ivies," and giddy over the prospect of at least one of their children
making it out of Florida, they had pressured him not to take a football
scholarship to a place back home. At times, Wade's anger, even the
spittle flying out of his mouth, seemed noble to me. Or refreshing, at
least. On my first day at Columbia three kids who had known each
other for years at Horace Mann (or maybe it was Fieldston or Dalton
or Trinity) informed me, "We've decided you're intriguing and we'd
like to adopt you for a day." Between that and Wade, not a hard call.

But mostly, Wade's act was tedious. I shouldn't call it an act. It wasn't
shtick exactly. His anger was real. Deeply felt. But it was dressed up
in an act that came right off the rack, right down to the cigarette behind his ear and the rolled-up sleeves. Do kids these days still idolize
James Dean? In the early eighties they still did. I had my own phase for
a few months in tenth grade, when I covered my walls with posters of
him, slicked my hair back, and fantasized about driving a Porsche 550
Spyder, the car he died in. *For a few months in tenth grade.* But Wade,
who had been held back a year at some point and so was at least
nineteen by now, still hadn't kicked the habit. Deep in his cups at a bar
on Broadway near 111th Street called the Marlin (which closed in the
late nineties and is now Mel's Burger Bar), he was often heard to say,
to whoever was sitting next to him or no one in particular, "Have you
ever seen *Rebel Without a Cause*, directed by Nicholas Ray?" People
usually assumed it was some kind of devious rhetorical question, or
mysterious mind-fuck, or just a trap to get them to admit to being
middlebrow, and ignored it.

Was hanging out with Wade tedious? Absolutely. But it was also
exciting in its way, because it was inconceivable that Wade could sus-

tain this level of simplemindedness for much longer before people were onto him and something bad happened. How long can an angry young man for whom *Rebel Without a Cause* is an inspiration survive with his ego intact (and without assaulting someone) in a place where kids from New York private schools who have known each other since kindergarten are banding together and adopting people for a day?

The answer is *less than one semester*. Early one morning in early December of 1986, after punching a kid who'd called him "beyond ridiculous," he called a number from the *Village Voice* classifieds, bought a used Harley from the man who answered the phone, a few days later got a tattoo of the Harley on his shoulder (and a few days after that the phrase "The bike stops here" tattooed in cursive beneath it), and then dropped out of college and took off. "The bike stops here" was supposed to be a pun on "The buck stops here," but it made no sense. What he meant to say is the bike is *starting* here. *Wherever I am is the beginning of an adventure.* That, as he explained to me after sobering up and realizing his mistake, is what he'd had in mind.

And that's just what he did. In December 1986 Wade embarked on a life of what most people (or at least those of us who don't recoil from the hell of endless change) would characterize as *endless adventure*. And that's just the life he's been leading, give or take a few months here and there when he's been in rehab and a few years here and there when he's tried to go back to college in Florida, for almost three decades. No town or village or city or "hamlet" (a word he reserves for places where people are especially friendly to him) is off-limits. When you're six feet four inches, 260 pounds, and good with your hands, it's not hard to move around a lot, finding odd jobs wherever you go, and when you're wounded-looking to boot (a little scary, but mostly cuddly), odd beds to crash in as well.

What is Wade searching for exactly? I have no idea. I barely know the man. I spent a dozen nights at the Marlin during my first semester of college watching him gradually lose his bearings and have seen him only sporadically since then. All that I can attest to is a short attention span, a knack for mumbling, a love of women and movies and beer (preferably Beck's or Heineken), and a need for affirmation, for whenever he arrives in a new place and sets up what he perceives to be solid stakes, he sends out a long letter, part screed, part manifesto, to just about everyone he knows, with lots of *italics* and underlinings and ALL CAPS, and some bold for good measure just in case you're dozing off, proclaiming and protesting and pontificating about how happy he is in the place he's moved to, and how much *fuckin' better* the place he's moved to is than New York City. And not just *fuckin' better* but very often a HUNDRED TIMES *fuckin' better*, and in addition to being a HUNDRED TIMES *fuckin' better* there's often a BONUS benefit that he tacks on just in case you didn't get the point. "The music scene in New Orleans, not to mention the food scene there, is a HUNDRED TIMES *fuckin' better* than the music scene in New York City, and the BONUS is that it's more authentic"; "Driving the open roads of western Pennsylvania is a HUNDRED TIMES more soothing than a class at Jivamukti, and the BONUS is that it's cheaper"; "The chicks in Vancouver are a HUNDRED TIMES hotter than the chicks in New York City, and the BONUS is that they don't feel a need to act like it"; the club scene in Madrid, the subways in DC, the farmer's market wherever, everything everywhere else is a HUNDRED TIMES *fuckin' better* because New York City, for all the OBVIOUS reasons, *fuckin' sucks*.

But there's a catch. Within two or three years Wade's always back. *Back in New York City*. And he always seems pretty happy to be here, going to free punk shows in Gowanus and free movies at the Museum of the Moving Image and more free movies in Bryant Park, and filling his belly on free hors d'oeuvres at Fairway and Zabar's, and free beer at this or that opening or premiere or after-party. "New York rules!" he once screamed in a moment of weakness. "There is more free stuff here than anywhere else!" And then some girlfriend dumps him, and he has nowhere to sleep, and he takes off again. And then a letter will arrive from the "hamlet" of Seattle, where he managed to shack up for six months with a graduate student in biostatistics at the University of Washington, and where the coffee is a HUNDRED TIMES more pure and flavorful and reliably organic than it is in New York City.

Getting these letters from Wade over the years has been super soothing for me. Taken as a whole, they've been the best argument I've ever heard for why New York City, where I've lived off and on for the last twenty-eight years, and where you can get just about anything free if you really look for it, is a hundred times better than anywhere else.

Except for *one letter*, which he sent me eight years ago, and a very small portion of which I found surprisingly moving. Deeply buried in a few thousand words of dreck was a tiny nugget of profundity. Wade had managed, as if digging for gold with a backhoe, to come up with something beautiful and true, and what surprised me in part was that I hadn't come up with it on my own. For over twenty years it had been staring me in the face, and yet I hadn't seen it. I felt that I had been *scooped*. Not so much intellectually scooped as emotionally scooped. Even spiritually scooped. And by a guy who had no business scooping me on any level at all.

The subject heading of his email was HOUSE PARTIES IN LA BLOW DOORS ON HOUSE PARTIES IN NEW YORK. The email was divided into five categories: Bathrooms, Neighbors, Spending the Night, Hooking Up, and then a fifth and final catchall category that included Jacuzzi, Garage, Rec-Room; Patio; Lawn; Guesthouse; Driveway; and Eucalyptus Trees. Most of his argument for why house parties in LA blow doors on house parties in New York had nothing at all specifically to do with LA. Pretty much all he was saying was that parties in big nice houses are more fun than parties in small crummy apartments. Under the heading "Bathrooms," for instance, he basically just said that partying in a house with lots of bathrooms is more fun than in an apartment with only one bathroom, because you never have to wait in line, and even if there were a line, the BONUS is that you could go to the bathroom in the bushes outside. Under "Neighbors," he said that since there is more distance between houses than there is between apartments, namely a whole side yard full of tall trees between them and not just a thin wall, there is a much smaller chance the neighbors will call the cops.

The tiny nugget of profundity was located in the final, catchall category, specifically under the subheading "Patio." The word meant a lot to him for many reasons. For example, he liked what the word did to his mouth when he said it. "PA-TI-O, PA-TI-O, PA-TI-O," he wrote. "Look in the mirror. Say it slowly. Syllable by syllable by syllable. It starts with a smile, and ends with a kiss." He was clearly proud of this imagery, but it was labored. Look in the mirror and say *PA-TI-O* slowly, syllable by syllable by syllable, and only by contorting your mouth into a rictus on *PA*, then pursing your lips on the letter *O* like you're sucking on a gobstopper soaked in vinegar, will you get anything resembling a smile or kiss out of this.

The more inspiring part of Wade's patio riff had to do with what he called the *symbolic power* of a patio. To communicate this power to the reader, Wade fell back on a free-associative style that I would normally find hard to take, but in this case, since it came from the heart and veered as close to poetry as Wade will likely ever get, I found myself, despite my best efforts to be irritated, in sympathy with him, *at one with him*, adoring him and in awe of him for letting himself go, for giving himself up to it, to *love*, and to the force of his lyricism (and to be frank, to the force of his logorrhea as well; I admire people who aren't so clenched up and constipated that they won't run at the mouth when the spirit moves them), and for unleashing on the world this wild, beautiful, soulful description of him weaving his way through the living room of a crowded party in Pacific Palisades, in the early evening of a Saturday in summer, drink in his left hand, and thinking that he had maybe exhausted all the party had to offer, that there was no one beautiful or cool or interesting left to meet and he would just cut his losses and go home, *but then suddenly turning to my right*, and seeing, through giant sliding glass doors, a big wide-open patio full of lots of new people, and how excited he is, like a high school kid sneaking out of his bedroom window to go to a keg party at the beach, at the promise of a *whole other party outside*, and how the patio is a LINK to the *lawn beyond the patio*, where there's even more people, and a LINK to the *sky beyond the lawn*, a sky full of seagulls and treetops and fading sunlight, and when I grab hold of the handle of the sliding glass door with my right hand and slide it open, the sound reminds me of the LOW RUMBLE OF A DISTANT TRAIN and the *warm promise of arrival* at something fresh and new and wonderful, and yeah how the energy in LA is CENTRIFUGAL, because *a patio pulls you out and through and beyond where you were before*, as opposed to the energy in New York City which is so obviously CENTRIPETAL, like the flush of a toilet, and you're tethered and you're tight and you're hemmed in here, you're looking down at your feet instead of up at the sky, you hide in your buildings and your brownstones and your shitty walk-ups, buildings that block out the light and send you underground. New York City *looms over you*, shuts you down, while Cali *opens you up*. And why? Because of the PATIO!!!

Reading that letter from Wade made me really miss Southern California, where I grew up, and where I've been moving back to, from New York City, always saying goodbye, for about as long as I've known Wade. I always come back to the city, because it's a hundred times fuckin' better than any other place (free movies, free concerts, free hors d'oeuvres at Fairway and Zabar's, *so much stuff here is free!*), but for the rest of my life I'll keep moving back to LA, for as little as two weeks, whatever it takes to get a fix, and now I know why: because HOUSE PARTIES IN LA BLOW DOORS ON HOUSE PARTIES IN NEW YORK. And the BONUS? When you're hooking up, you don't have to take a cab home to seal the deal, like you do in New York, which so often kills the mood; you can just finish what you started right there on the lawn or in the guesthouse or in the Jacuzzi.

THE CITY, HOARDED

Colin Harrison

L et us please agree from the outset that I suffer a kind of disease. The words "hobby" or "obsession" or even "mania" seem too insignificant to me, for these are mere passing conditions, and what I have will never leave me. Yes, *disease* will do just fine. What is that disease? I collect maps of New York City—the whole city, parts of the city, the city in the seventeenth, eighteenth, nineteenth, twentieth, and twenty-first centuries. The city as it was built and rebuilt and planned to be built and never built. The city in peace and war (Revolutionary, Civil, World War II, and 9/11), the city in prosperity and depression. The city as rendered in engraved copper plate, in lithograph, in offset printing. The city as early Dutch settlement, as fortified trading post, as pre-industrial port, as manufacturing gigantus, as global destination with dozens of transatlantic ocean liners arriving and leaving every day, as arterial automobile ganglia designed by Robert Moses, as a klieg-light confection created by radio and movies and television and now Internet, as their wish and my idea and your dream.

All these visions and versions swim and separate and recombine in the head of a crazy person who wants to see and, if possible, remember every map of New York ever made. Who wants to see the city historic as its footpaths and original streams and ponds disappear beneath proliferating dirt roadways into a relentless grid of fire districts and neighborhoods and colored subway and bus lines and ethnic enclaves and as marked by rates of dysentery and locations of churches and bars and poorhouses and sewer lines and parks and railyards and skyscrapers and police stations. You can see *all* of these things in my maps of the city. This is why I gather them, I stack them, I devour them. I want them, but what a pedestrian word, *want*. Useless in these circumstances. I desire and need and require maps of New York City, I crave them, I fever for them, I feel that a map I do not have but want is yet rightfully mine; I must touch them and smell them and possess them, must run my finger along their stiff or soft or irregular damaged edges. The paper brittle or yellowed or oxidized with rust foxing. Or torn or repaired. Or folded so many times the creases have given way to nothing. But every map has something! *There* is the crooked first demarcation of "Broad-Way," *there* is a serrated line denoting where Central Park may someday be built, *there* is the location of the Twin Towers when they stood. I must have these many pieces of paper. Whatever ostensible refinement I may have only goes so deep, and beneath that there is something else—harder, meaner, a map collector governed by covetous greed, prudence be damned.

I live in a brownstone in Brooklyn, and many of its walls are covered with framed maps of New York City. There is, for example, an early map of the first subway lines. And Brooklyn in the 1850s, when its eastern frontier was still a smattering of farming villages growing together into one entity. And one depicting where the British and the Revolutionary armies have recently battled in the year 1776. There is a huge colored map of Midtown from the 1960s, showing literally every building. And so on, dozens. The members of my family have been exceedingly tolerant about the relentless crawl of maps up and down the walls, following the stairwells, snaking around corners and along hallways. To be specific, there are maps of New York on the walls of the ground-floor foyer, hallway, guest room, and bathroom, and my office (more on that in a moment). Taking the stairwell to the first floor, one passes many maps, and then finds more in the dining room, the first-floor bathroom, the first-floor foyer and hall. The stairwell to the second floor has maps, and they give way briefly to a hallway of family photographs before resuming in the master bedroom and then up the stairs to the third floor, where their spread has been battled against heroically by various family members. But there are small gaps here and there and sooner or later, I will have my way. Left purely to my own devices, I would have framed maps from my collection cover every inch of wall space in the house.

I collect maps in a half dozen or so major categories: New York City proper—Manhattan; lower Manhattan; Midtown Manhattan, especially whimsical tourist maps from the mid-twentieth century; Brooklyn; and Long Island (with New York attached). I have so many Brooklyn maps that I prevailed upon my children's school in Brooklyn to accept a sizeable collection of them, for display. My Long Island maps by themselves number enough that they have started to crawl across the walls of our house in Long Island.

Now then, returning to my "office." It's not an office. It's a lost room in the New York Public Library. It is stuffed with maps. Don't ask me how many because I do not know. There are hundreds, certainly, maybe a thousand. Maybe more. I have been collecting maps of New York City a long time now. My maps are stacked in boxes and laid out flat in protective sleeves and kept in long tubes by the dozen, most scrawled with an identification ("1847 lower Manhattan, good"). They are *not* well organized. They are the product of one who must have more of them. Who is always looking. I have bookmarked the websites of every major and many minor map dealers around the country on my computer. I have cruised through and lurked and hovered in all the major map and rare book dealers in New York City. I have maps I bought years ago and have never seen since. Most people don't realize that there is a huge and chaotic market of New York maps on eBay. At any given time, several thousand are for sale. It is rare—very rare—when I have not seen all of them before. Perhaps once or twice a year I see something I haven't seen before. Most are worthless, but occasionally one comes along that is fabulous. There are others like me who lurk on eBay, waiting to strike. And we do. What else? I have spent innumerable hours tracking down maps in books sold by rare book dealers who may or may not know what they are selling. (So thrilling to find a toothsome map one craves in an old book, close the covers, then innocently ask what the cost is.) I have made inquiries as far away as Germany and Japan. I have met other collectors who are selling, one a man who lived in his nursing home room with his maps and little else. I have made cash transactions with a fellow who seems to know when every public library in North America is deaccessioning their books about or maps of New York. I have tracked down fabulous maps of New York that were printed in old daily or weekly newspapers. Then one has to find the rare newspaper dealer who sells that particular day and hope he doesn't know what he is selling. Here's an example. Al Hirschfeld, the long-lived caricaturist of Broadway and Hollywood who etched his daughter Nina's name in each portrait, once drew a map of New York City that appeared in the *New York Times* before World War II. Very few people know that. Even fewer have a copy of that map, as I do. *A disease.*

I was born in New York City, at Riverside Hospital, now gone, in 1960. My father was a student at Teachers College at Columbia. My mother was a very beautiful young actress who was trying to make her way acting in off-Broadway roles and the occasional television soap opera. They lived on 122nd Street between Broadway and Amsterdam in a big old apartment building. My uncle lent them $5,000 to buy an apartment. You could do that then. We moved to Philadelphia when I was six. But the spore of New York City was in me already, and some homing instinct carried me back in my midtwenties. I've lived in Brooklyn since 1987, and in my house since 1989. The things that happen to people have happened to me in New York. Birth, death, work, success, failure, love, fury, good meals, bad parties, muggings, you name it. Everything happened at a certain spot, a place on the map, my map of the city. Gradually I began to see signifiers and memories of my life contained within maps of New York City, old and new and very old. This happens to anyone who lives in New York for any amount of time. You begin to map yourself to the city even as the city itself is always changing in front of you and beneath you and above you. It is alive, you are alive. My first map went up on the wall in about 1992. The rest is craziness, *disease*.

Some people speculate in rare maps, for rare maps are now seen as a legitimate hedge against inflation the same way that collectible coins or fine art were first bought to diversify investment portfolios. But collectors, like me, are different. It's a fiendish little world, we greedily obsessive hoarders, we fetishizers of ancient ink and paper; we may see each other at the map-collecting societies, we trail through the overpriced Manhattan galleries asking casually if the runners have found anything interesting in the estate auctions in New England, the South, the Midwest. Whether anything extraordinary has turned up lately. As it *always* does, sooner or later!

Other than the wish to know one's own place, what drives such fanaticism? The end of paper. People have always collected maps, but now the world feels a great silent death transpiring. It is said that young Chinese moguls are buying up maps of China, especially the eastern coast, where so much has changed over the last thirty years—rivers moved, shorelines filled in, mountains pulverized. American collectors from the West tend to like the huge multicolored maps of Texas, with its shifting borders and adjacent lands marked as the territories of Apache or Comanche Indians, and, most especially, the priceless maps prior to 1740 that show the golden land of California as an island. But across the world, the common element is the demise of paper. Now maps are pure digital information, ever more brilliantly interactive sat-photo hybrids, ever more brilliantly interactive and throbbingly detailed. Zoom in, zoom out. But no matter how dense they are with glittering up-to-the-minute information, these maps are not tangible. No practiced hand has made them. No weak-eyed wretch has pressed an irregular sheet of rag paper upon an ink-rolled copper plate. I can't touch them or feel them; continuously updated, they preserve *nothing*.

So, against this onslaught of time, I collect maps of New York City. And, admittedly, the New York my maps hold has been lost to all living memory. I can only console myself by inspecting them closely. I gaze at such maps, then lift my eyes to the window, to the mind's eye, and see what has become of those same places, the glass city built atop the iron city built atop the brick city built over wooden structures held together with pegs and four-sided nails. For that is what New York is, a never-completed masterwork, torn down even as it is resurrected, each minute populated by a different swarm of humanity streaming in and out.

Stare too long, dream too hard, and one loses oneself, falls into the map itself. Look, please look, at my 1824 Hooker plan of lower Manhattan. Here is Blackwell's Island, later bluntly called Welfare Island, now named Roosevelt Island, running along the east side of Manhattan, a slender pilot-fish to the great whale itself; I can see the workhouse, the hospital for incurables, the lunatic asylum, the women's alms house, the smallpox hospital. My eyes drop down to the southern tip of Manhattan, the part of the city that has changed the most over time. How I wish to stand at the end of the stone walkway that led over the water out to the battery of canons that once protected the city's harbor and watch the wooden vessels creak past, knowing what was coming in the future, how the water between the Battery and Manhattan would be filled in and built upon, the whole jagged blade-tip of the island smoothed and rounded by thousands of ant men laboring over the decades. I have dreamed of descending downward from the never-taken satellite images of the nineteenth-century city, the street grid smudged by the parallel plumes of smoke from thousands of chimneys and stacks, down, down, down until I can see the clippers, schooners, catboats, and brigs chaotically busy in the harbor, closer until the narrow streets became perceptible, muddy and horse-clogged with the many black dots moving to and fro on the sidewalks being the dusty bowlers of the men and dodgy boys going about their dodgy business, the larger and fewer multicolored shapes being of course the Manhattan ladies dressed in hats and fine dresses—

—oh, idiocy, oh disease, oh love.

ALL I REALLY NEED TO KNOW I LEARNED IN NEW YORK CITY

Whoopi Goldberg

T he first time I went to Europe, I visited Germany with my boy-friend, who had family there. I was very young and hadn't been many places—this was way before I was famous. As soon as we arrived, I had this incredible revelation. "Oh, my God," I said to his family, "I know all about this area! The food, the language. I know all about the *Schwarzwald,*" the Black Forest. They were stunned. "How do you know about this?" they asked in disbelief. And I was like, "*Please.* I'm from Chelsea."

That was the first time it dawned on me how much I knew about the rest of the world, and how prepared I was for it, just from growing up in New York City—that I had been *everywhere* before I'd ever actually gone anywhere.

I grew up in the Chelsea Projects, 288 Tenth Avenue at Twenty-Sixth Street. A lot of kids there were first-generation Americans with immigrant parents who were still speaking Yiddish or Chinese or Spanish or Portuguese or Russian, or just name a language and they were speaking it. You had to be able to speak a smattering of every-thing to be able to say, in the language of the parents, "Hello, Mrs. So-and-so. Is So-and-so at home? Can she come out to play?" You ate every conceivable food from the rest of the world there. You were exposed to all different kinds of traditions.

It wasn't just the projects. The whole city was a classroom—a big, fun, exciting classroom. All over town, you learned stuff you didn't even know you were learning. You didn't have to be rich to learn it either. My mom was a teacher—a great Head Start teacher—and she made sure I partook of everything New York had to offer people who didn't have any money, because she knew it was the greatest education in the world.

I'll never forget when the World's Fair came to Flushing Meadows Park in 1964 and 1965. The theme was "Peace Through Understanding," and that was the first place anyone ever saw "It's a Small World." If you lived in New York City, that was true—it *was* a small world. The logo for the fair was blue and orange. To this day, any time I see those colors together, it means the World's Fair to me. There was also Freedomland USA, a sort of Wild West US history–themed amusement park in the Bronx. That was the craziest place!

We went to all the museums, which were free back then. In the summertime, we'd go on the Circle Line, and over to Liberty Park, and my mom would have us walk all the way up to the Statue of Liberty's crown. Or we'd take the train to the beach in Rockaway or Coney Island. One of my favorite memories in life is when my mom would say to my brother and me, "Okay, you guys, I thought we might go to Coney Island today." I loved Coney Island so much. We'd pack sandwiches, walk to Eighth Avenue, and get on the train to Brooklyn. When the train came out into the daylight, I remember tingling with excitement. It was like, *We are on our way to Coney Island!*

There was so much I could do on my own too. I was independent from a very young age. Back then, the world felt safer. As a kid, you could leave the house at nine a.m. and not see your parents until six p.m., and they'd never say, "Where the hell were you?" Your parents would put you out of the house to get fresh air, and they didn't want you back in the house until dinnertime. They didn't want you sitting around when there was *so much* out there. They wanted you going to the museums or to Central Park: that was the people's park. You could ride the carousel there or have picnics and listen to music on the lawn or, in the winter, go ice-skating. (I still love going to the park, maybe sitting down there with a slice of real New York pizza or a hot dog from Gray's Papaya. Those hot dogs have snap to them!)

You could ride the bus for five cents right on up to Lincoln Center, before it was Lincoln Center. You could watch dancers dancing there, getting ready for *West Side Story* before they performed that night. You could see famous people walking down the street in New York. We would just wave and say "Hey!" and if you were lucky, they'd say "Hey!" back. If you were a walker, which is what I was, you could walk up to Forty-Third Street and watch actors leaving the theater. You could see James Earl Jones, or you could see Elizabeth Taylor and Richard Burton dashing into their car. In my neighborhood I'd see Rip Torn and Geraldine Page—that's where they lived. It was very exciting.

Now I'm the one who gets accosted when I'm walking down the street or when I'm hanging out in Central Park. But people are okay with me. They're respectful. They'll wave and say "Hey," or they'll come up and ask me for my autograph. And most of the time, I give it to them. I was taught very early on that it's a big deal when somebody comes up to ask for your autograph. It's taken them a good ten minutes to work up the nerve to talk to you. And they're thinking, "Oh my God, I hope they are the person I want them to be." I really do try to be the person they hoped I would be.

And I like to think I'm the same person I became as I grew up here. New York City played a big part in making me who I am. It's where I learned that I could pursue whatever I loved but that I couldn't be a slacker, because everybody else here was hustling. People are hustling at their jobs, hustling on the train. Musicians give you concerts in the subway station. There are artists who are hustling their work outside. If you want to make it in this town, you can't fuck off. You have to be present. You have to keep moving.

And you have to do it with your head up. Because if your head is down, you walk into people. You keep your head up, like you own the street. Like, "That's right, I'm from New York."

Besides, if your head is down, you miss everything. Things change, and you don't notice—don't notice that they finally finished the West Side Highway (I am grateful they did because it seemed like it took ninety years to do it!), don't notice that the hospital you were born in is gone (I was born in Saint Vincent's), don't notice that there are no more carriage rides around Central Park. (I will miss those. When I was growing up, whenever something good happened, you did that. Whenever you wanted to show that you cared about somebody, you took them in the carriage. That's what you did. You went *clippity-clop*.)

New York is a vibrant city. It's everything you've heard it is. It's crazy, it's horrible, it's magnificent, it's beautiful. It's hard to become a real grown-up in, because it really lends itself to a good time. It's a real live wire, hard to leave, like a living, breathing entity in your life. Since the 1600s, New York City has been communicating with everyone who comes here, putting out information. Like, "Hey, we're New York, and this is how we do things. Come if you want to. But don't be surprised when you get sucked in."

NEW YORK THREE TIMES

Alexander Chee

I moved to New York for the first time in the fall of 1991. I boarded a bus in San Francisco with some of my possessions and a copy of Robert Graves's *The White Goddess*, in which he posits that all literature is only great if it focuses on stories of the Goddess—good reading for a cross-country trip. I did the trip dressed in jean cutoffs, combat boots, and a sleeveless hoodie. I didn't know this was the book written by the same author as the original *Goodbye to All That*, the memoir Graves wrote of his experiences during the First World War, the title of which Joan Didion would use for her famous essay on leaving New York. What I knew was that I was still something of a lapsed witch, trying to feel my way into the future and writing, and New York was a place I remembered mostly from college, when I had gone there on weekends to test my looks on the men of the city. This book was considered a curiosity of a kind, the literary equivalent of a garden folly, and I wanted to understand it.

When I got off that bus, I don't know how much I understood of *The White Goddess,* but I went straight to meet my friend Eliza, my future roommate, who had rented an apartment for us in a neighborhood she swore was the cheapest of the New York neighborhoods—

Williamsburg, at that time. She had found us a two-bedroom on Berry between South Fourth and South Fifth, almost under the Williamsburg Bridge, for four hundred a month—which we split. There was a burned-out shell of a diner around the corner from us that looked dangerous to eat at (it would eventually become a restaurant called Diner) and a Dominican deli with that coffee that was stronger than cocaine (this is still there). The streets would fill with the little vials of crack discarded by the prostitutes waiting for the truckers, or by the truckers—who could tell?—and I remember that first night I slept restlessly, fearing the cracking sounds were gunshots, when really they were the metal sheets on the bridge, laid over the holes in the roadway, snapping each time they were hit.

In the morning I discovered the layer of soot that always would fall there, coming off the bridge like a black rain.

The city I found then was beautiful old buildings covered in graffiti, nightclubs open past dawn, drag queens dancing on bars in wigs lit by Christmas lights, house music, Greek diners open twenty-four hours, and Puerto Rican and Dominican bodegas selling coffee so sweet it made your teeth hurt. I fell in love with it all, but most important to me were the bookstores and magazine shops where I could linger for hours, read something I had never seen before and might never see again, and it would change me, and I was glad.

This is why you came to live in New York, I told myself.

That, and a man I had fallen in love with, who would change me also. And for which I mostly would be glad.

At some point during my first year there, I remembered that definition of Roman fever in the famous story by Edith Wharton—that it was about falling in love with old things, the ancient world. For Americans, New York was one of those places.

By the time I moved away in a year, I would be packing my boxes in another apartment altogether, a block off Fort Greene Park. A lot had happened, and it felt like too much and not enough. I had nearly broken up with the man I'd moved to New York for, had held three jobs—as a bookseller at A Different Light Books, a barback at Crobar, and the assistant editor at *Out* magazine. I'd also caught hep A—it was going around the city—and after a terrible weekend in Woodhull Hospital, in a room with a smear of blood on the wall from the previous patient, never cleaned up, I went back to my mother's home in Maine for three weeks to recover.

My Williamsburg apartment wasn't working out, so when I got back from Maine, I moved to the spare room of a painter who at the time was making work with his own blood and semen. In retrospect, that Woodhull blood smear seems like some strange omen of my next home, one I was unable to read. The painter would pick men up in the park and bring them in, walking by the kitchen door, where I'd be writing on my typewriter, introducing them each time by name as if I would ever see them again, and each time I would nod and act as if I would see them again also, like in a Noh play about cruising for sex. I typed up the stories I used to apply for the Iowa Writers' Workshop in that kitchen, and then I got in, and now I was moving away, though that kitchen felt lucky for writing and I was sorry to leave it.

I had set two goals for myself that year: to get a magazine job and to get into graduate school on a fellowship. I'd accomplished both, but I also sensed that somehow New York had made it possible. Living among all those old things had cast a spell on me that made something new—for me at least—happen.

And so, with my boyfriend, who was also off to an MFA program— UA Tucson—I loaded up a car. And as we drove west, I remember thinking, I'm not done with you, New York City. See you soon.

• • •

I returned in 1994. During those two years of graduate school, New York was always home, and when my relationship fell apart, I knew I was still going back there.

"I'm gay and I'm single," I told people. "Where else am I going to go?"

I moved into a three-bedroom on the Upper West Side, with a sunken living room and a fireplace, a block off Central Park. I was setting up house with my brother and sister, both younger—my brother had just gotten a job on Wall Street as an analyst, my sister was starting at Columbia as a freshman. Our mother had just gone bankrupt, and given our collapsing family finances, we decided somehow it would be a good idea for us to all live together in the city.

Unlike many families, we liked each other.

We were like a Korean version of the Glass family but without the parents, Salinger but Amerasian. Our landlady was an ancient and terrifying woman who we discovered had been on the cover of the *New York Post* twice—once for having run a deposit check scam, and the second time for having tried to order a hit on a relative. I had no idea why she was free, but she was and would often be out front, asking us how things were, as if she were waiting for what would happen after six months: unable to afford the rent, we moved out in the middle of the night.

In my memory, that apartment was like the strange gate to the rest of what happened, a period during which my smart, hardworking sister, recruited by nightlife promoters—she was and is a beauty—was soon going to the most exclusive clubs in the city and drinking for free. Soon she was working the door to downtown clubs, telling people she was Samoan so no one would mess with her. Samoan gangs are famously the most violent, she explained: "If they think my brothers are Samoan gangsters, they won't bother me."

She was still going to Columbia and making good grades, but she had a new, somewhat unnerving sophistication, littering the bathroom with Patricia Fields minis and lipsticks of many kinds.

My brother meanwhile had been working making nothing on cold calls until he joined a little-known firm at the time named Blackstone as an analyst. He was there so much that his bosses would say, "You're here when we get here and you're here when we leave, so far as we know you haven't left the building." He had two suits that first year, bought at J. Crew and altered at a tailor's so they'd seem better than they were.

And I had trained as a waiter, while working on my first novel.

I had the nervous collapse most MFA graduates have. A section of a novel I sent to *The New Yorker* hadn't gotten published but it had gotten me the attention of an editor at William Morrow, which had gotten me my first agent. She thought the novel I wanted to finish was going to be too big: "No one wants to publish a six-hundred-page novel," she said. And when William Morrow passed, I would decide to write what I referred to as "a fucking autobiographical novel like everyone else" and begin work on what would become my first novel, *Edinburgh*.

We left that apartment very changed, I think—we had somehow set the foundations of who we'd all later become. My sister will always be a little more glamorous than most yoga teachers, for example. My brother left Blackstone before returning to work there again, as an executive. And me, well, I finished that novel.

The departure from the Upper West Side apartment became its own kind of adventure, two years of temporary places. I couch-surfed for the first few months—first back to Williamsburg, then to the East Village—before finally getting a sublet in Park Slope that convinced me to stay out there. I got my first lease on my own in 1996, but it was only after almost two years of having sublet all over the city—East Village, West Village, Gramercy, Sugar Hill, Chelsea—and to this day I'll pass a neighborhood and a flood of memories will come back, hidden until I turn the corner. The roommate who was a "masseuse," the entire box of jewelry I left in the back of a cab, the fellow waiter I lived with whom I was desperately in love with, the friend whose cat I gave away mistakenly, having misread his letter from London—and the many men, always, who had kept me company in all these places. A face will stop me on the street, and I'll wonder if it's this one or that one, but it doesn't matter, not at all.

The first real apartment I landed with a lease was in Park Slope and came with a rider giving it to me at five hundred dollars below market value for reasons no one would explain. I'd later learn this sort of agreement is something the landlord installs to destabilize the rent sooner when the market comes back, but I don't think he did it right. At the time, I could only think it had been the site of a terrible crime or suicide. I found it quite placid, actually; it had a muddy yard I turned into a rose garden. The landlord would spend many years trying to send me leases without the rider, and each time I would call and tell him the good news that his rent stabilization was still in effect, complete with tax breaks, and could he send me the corrected lease? And so it went, for eight years, until 2004, when I moved away to Los Angeles.

I was leaving because I had said I would only leave New York if a bag of money fell on me. By now I had published my first novel, and the year I moved to Los Angeles, I had won both a Whiting Award and an NEA fellowship in fiction. The idea of spending that money on the Rube Goldberg machine that was New York broke my heart in advance of doing it. And so, with two bags of money having fallen on me, I was making good on my promise to myself and leaving.

"Everyone is moving to LA," the UPS guy said to me, as he weighed my boxes on Seventh Avenue in the Slope.

"Really?" I said.

"You're the third guy this week," he said. This felt like its own kind of warning. I didn't take it, though. I was tired of New York, I had decided. To stay seemed likely to doom me to some existence in which I was forever trying at and failing at the life I wanted to live in New York. "This city is just a guide to my exes," I told someone. This because the last four men I had dated had turned into two couples—one of those couples still married to this day.

"It's hard to meet people in LA," everyone would say, as if it would stop me.

"Do you promise?" I'd reply each time. "I'm only going if it's true." I was tired of the endless run-ins on the street: each time someone asked me how the writing was going, they had no idea they were the second, third, fourth person to ask it. I wanted the opposite of street life. I wanted urban solitude, days and days when I would run into only strangers. And so I left and moved to LA.

I told myself I was tired of New York, but I was tired of the story I lived there. I wasn't tired of New York. Much in the way New York remained my home when I was in graduate school, even when I turned away from it and moved to Los Angeles, I could never find a barber there who cut my hair like the Tajik barber in the East Village who had cut my hair for a decade. I found I felt as if I didn't look like myself when he didn't cut my hair.

I told myself if there was ever an apartment that was going to get me over New York, it was the four-thousand-square-foot apartment in the Talmadge, the Koreatown building built for a silent movie queen, Norma Talmadge, by her husband, who feared she would miss New

York so much that she would leave him and go back. It was built to exactly resemble a New York prewar building, and it does, so much so that it is often used for location filming. The lease was held by an old flame who worked in film and television production, and he lived there with several friends. I became one of them, moving into a one-bedroom suite with a walk-in closet, making my coffee in the butler kitchen, writing in the old maid's quarters, wandering the massive library, and watching television in the vast living room for seven months, until it was time to move on.

I used to laugh at the irony of how I had moved to this kind of building by way of leaving New York. I may have been the last person to learn it was just a cover for the way I didn't really want to leave New York, which was its own lesson, learned in the six years ahead.

I stayed in Los Angeles until the grant money ran out, then went to Maine, where I lived in my mom's basement until I could sell a book proposal and earn some money, then moved to Rochester, for a man again, an academic who had taken a job at a small Catholic college. I spent a year there as what I call a disgruntled faculty spouse before heading to Amherst College as their "visiting writer."

"How long is the visit?" people would ask. "Four years," I would say. "Long visit," they'd say. "Not for Amherst College," I'd say.

Once I was in Amherst, I encouraged my friends back in New York to treat me as if I lived in the outermost borough of Manhattan, the Amtrak train just a gussied-up subway train from Penn Station to Amherst. H&H bagels came up on it every day for the bakery I frequented. Most of the people there had spent time in New York, either as students or adults, and I joked it was as if the dog people of Park Slope had moved away to make a town.

I made frequent trips to the city, on the generous travel budget afforded to professors there, and always timed to literary events. I eventually decided I would move back when my term was done.

In the last year of my term, I fell in love with a man who lived in New York. When I told him on one of my visits that I was going to go apartment hunting, he said, "No, you're not." I live there in that apartment with him still.

I went to get coffee in Williamsburg with a friend the other day who was telling me of how after three months away, she couldn't quite get back into the habit of living here again and she felt like she was going to move away. We spoke of a party we weren't going to go to and then walked to a new park by the water.

That first apartment I lived in on Berry Street is now probably six to ten thousand dollars a month. We passed the new restaurants that had opened in the months she was away.

"Go look," she said, as we stood outside one of them. She had her dog and couldn't peek in. I did. It looked beautiful and shabby and old, as if something new had been born on top of something old without getting rid of all of it.

It looked like New York.

We went to the water. There was the incredible view, the soaring buildings, that strange metal Enchanted Forest into which we go, day after day, and never emerge unchanged, even if we just go out for dinner. She was alienated by the way the city had changed in just three months. I wondered if I felt the same.

"If I could be in awe of this place again," she said, "I think I could live here. But I don't live in that view."

I understood her. But I didn't feel that way.

I still live in that view.

New York is my home. I live in Hell's Kitchen in an unrenovated railroad apartment, rent-stabilized, on the second floor of a small building with a bar downstairs. Everyone around us pays three and four times our rent. Sometimes I hear the laughter of the bar patron I call the Cackler. Sometimes I smell the garlic knots from the pizzeria next door. I work out in a gym full of aging actors and dancers, all in incredible shape. I share a community garden plot with this man I fell in love with, where we grow herbs and roses, and every so often I come home to a rose he grew, in a tiny bud vase on my desk. Or he brings back the oregano from the garden, which is second only to the oregano I can get on the islands of Greece. And while sometimes the transformations I have been through here scare me to remember, that sense I had, of the way living among the oldest things turned me into who I became next—that is still true. It made me who I am; it will make me into who I become next.

Unlike my friend, I'm still in awe of New York. I still feel something when the Q emerges onto the bridge and we pass over the East River, and whatever day or night view there is emerges—the towers covered in light or full of it, the water below, the sky above. When I don't feel that little leap of the heart, that thrill that makes me look up from my book and look north and south to the sea, I'll know it's time to leave.

Until then, I live here.

THE MUSE OF THE COYOTE UGLY SALOON

Elizabeth Gilbert

*E*very time I've ever needed a refuge, New York City has taken me in. Which makes no sense because New York is supposed to be pretty much the exact opposite of that. New York is supposed to be the place that rejects you, that humbles you, that breaks your spirit and kicks your ass, that chews you up and then spits you out to freeze on the sidewalk like January's dog shit. Except that's never been my relationship with this town. To me, New York City is Mama. Every time I've ever knocked on its door—no matter what time of day, no matter what condition I've found myself—New York City opens to me. Smacks me upside the head a little bit on my way in, like, "What's the matter with you now, you big stupid dummy?" but always lets me in. Clears a space for me. Finds a bed for me. Makes room at the table.

Four times, I've moved to New York. Four completely different circumstances.

The first time, I came there for college, running into the city's embrace as fast as I could out of my small New England town. I was ignorant and innocent and I looked like an extra from Little House on the Prairie and I probably should have been the ultimate in mugger bait, but instead I got protected and educated by the city, and I found my tribe. I graduated and left town in 1991, eager to discover the world.

Except that the world messed me up. So the second time I moved to New York, I was twenty-four—heartbroken and disappointed in both life and love. I'd tried existing elsewhere on the planet, and things hadn't worked out so good for me. I was broke and depressed. I drove into the city with my battered 1966 Plymouth Fury and left it parked and unlocked on Fourteenth Street, accumulating tickets, until someone finally stole it. A friend gave me her couch for sleeping, till I could get on my feet. The Coyote Ugly Saloon gave me a job (which is what this essay is about). The bar gave me a husband. I got published. I became the writer I'd always dreamed of being. New York let me do all that. I got married and moved out to the suburbs, bought a big house.

The marriage bombed. The house became a prison. I ditched it all, and eight years later, New York City took me back again. No judgment. This city never judges me. No questions asked. The town took me in and allowed my sorrows to dissipate in the crowds. There's a safety in numbers, indeed, and that safety is the sense of endless privacy, endless strangers, endless possibilities for reinvention of the self. I moved to Hell's Kitchen. Nobody there cared about me or knew of my failings, and that was just perfect. My apartment was right over the entrance to the Lincoln Tunnel, noisy and dirty, and I slept there every night like an infant in a beautiful polluted bassinet. I pulled myself back together and gathered my senses. I went out in the world again, fell in love again, got married again, moved to the country, bought another big house.

Two years ago, my husband and I bought a small place in Manhattan. We kind of did it on the sly. We did it without getting rid of our home or each other, but it still felt like a hot, dirty secret, like we were having an affair together. This has been my fourth, and—I think—my final return to New York. This will be the eighth apartment I've inhabited in this city, but this time I'm going to keep it. We don't live in New York all the time and probably never will, but I've finally had to admit that I need a permanent escape hatch there, to transport me back to asylum when the rest of the world lets me down.

I like my rural life, with my garden and my neighbors. But in the same way that old bank robbers always keep a safe filled with guns and passports stashed in the back of their closet, I now keep a key to New York City tucked in my back pocket at all times. Just in case I need it at any moment. Just in case I ever have to pull off one last heist—rescuing myself from my choices once more, running home to the arms of Mama.

Even if it's just for the weekend.

I was not the prettiest bartender at the Coyote Ugly Saloon. In my opinion, that would have been Caroline. I was partial to Caroline, though, because she had been so nice to me when I began working here. She was very pretty and also very funny. When I asked Caroline how she'd gotten her first bartender job, she cupped her breasts and said simply, "These." (On first glance, however, Caroline's breasts didn't seem exceptional, and I said as much. She unzipped her bulky sweatshirt and showed them to me. Then I said, "Oh.")

Still, some regulars would have insisted that the prettiest bartender at the Coyote Ugly Saloon was Chris, who had sassy short hair like a boy's and a heart-stopping midriff. Of course, there was also Jackie to consider. Jackie was very pretty. Jackie was also famous for tossing shots of rum into her mouth, holding a lighter to her lips and blowing ten-foot bursts of flame across the room. There was definitely a cult of Jackie. Molly was pretty in a way that attracted the downtown crowd, and Dawn was pretty in the way that bikers like. And as for Jessie? Jessie was practically an objet d'art. Jessie was so goddamn pretty that it barely counted. One of the many regulars who fell in love with Jessie dated her a few times. She broke it off quickly. But he would still come into the Coyote Ugly Saloon every night, just to talk about her.

"Jessie was so beautiful," he would slur to some single woman drinking alone at the bar. "But she left me. She said I disgusted her. She told me she was repulsed by my touch."

After weeks of this, I finally said, "Listen, friend. You really need to work on a better pickup line. You really want to stop spreading that story around."

I gave a lot of good counsel at the Coyote Ugly Saloon. I certainly gave a lot of advice to men who'd fallen in love with their bartenders. It was a perennial problem. It was, after all, pretty much the whole point of the place.

When I was new at my bartending job, the owner of the Coyote Ugly Saloon told me, "If anyone ever comes into this place and asks for a mud slide, a zombie, or a grasshopper, go ahead and make the drink. Then charge the guy fifteen bucks for it. Then take him outside and beat the shit out of him. Because this is not that kind of bar."

Truly, the Coyote Ugly Saloon is not for everyone. If you do not like a bar where all the songs on the jukebox are either by Hank Williams or about Hank Williams, then you will not like this bar. It is loud and dark and hidden down low in the East Village of New York City.

If you had come into the Coyote Ugly Saloon when I was bartending and asked me for a martini, I would have poured you a shot of Jack Daniel's, and I would have said, "That's how we make martinis in this place, pal." If you had come into the Coyote Ugly Saloon when Caroline was bartending and asked her for a rusty nail, she might have climbed on top of the bar and poured the Jack Daniel's down your throat for you.

Now if you had come into the Coyote Ugly Saloon when Lil was bartending and asked, say, for a glass of water, you would have really been in trouble. Lil would have turned off the jukebox immediately. Lil would have climbed on top of the bar and shouted to the crowd, "Do we drink water in this goddamn bar?" And the crowd would have booed and laughed. Then Lil would have poured some Jack Daniel's down the throats of all your friends. Then Lil would have poured some Jack Daniel's down her own throat, and then Lil would have charged you for buying her a drink.

Liliana Lovell was my boss. She owns the Coyote Ugly Saloon.

Lil is short, cute, and tough. She has the body of a figure skater and the voice of a lifetime smoker. Lil is a legend in the neighborhood. She got her training across the street, at a bar called the Village Idiot, a dive that made the Coyote Ugly Saloon look like the Russian Tea Room. The Village Idiot was owned by this guy named Tom, who used to drink terrific amounts of Guinness and then piss behind his own jukebox. There were potholes in the floor of his bar deep enough to trip a horse. There was no drainage system, so the bartenders had to wade through shin-deep beer by the end of the night. When things started pressing in on them and the bartenders wanted to keep patrons back, they'd pour rum down the length of the bar and set it on fire. Tom hired only women bartenders at the Village Idiot. When Tom needed new help, he would put a sign outside reading, SHAMELESS SLUTS WANTED: NO EXPERIENCE NECESSARY.

Lil mastered her trade at the Village Idiot. She worked hard over there at Tom's bar. She saved up her tips—one greasy dollar bill at a time—and bought the Coyote Ugly Saloon. She opened her business right across the street from the Village Idiot. She was just twenty-five years old, two years older than I was, when she hired me to work in her bar.

Lil could drink with her customers until they were all blind, and then she'd make men suck tequila from her boots (and sometimes, I'm sorry to report, from her socks) while maintaining complete control. Lil was always in charge. Men loved her, but their love was tempered with a healthy touch of fear.

My favorite story from the canon of Lil goes like this: One night Lil traveled all the way to the Upper East Side to play pool at a snobbish tavern. An affluent-looking young man in a suit and tie made the unwise comment that women shouldn't be allowed to play pool, since they only got in the way of men. So Lil challenged the fellow and his friends to a game of pool. She ended up beating them three times in a row.

Humiliated, the young man claimed, "You're winning only because we've been drinking and you haven't."

Here he made his mistake.

"How many rounds of drinks have you had?" Lil asked.

"Four," the man said.

So Lil ordered herself five shots of Wild Turkey. She slammed the shots down, one after the other. Then Lil beat those little pricks once more just to teach them some manners.

Anyhow, that was my boss. I was afraid of her. I wanted to be her. I'd never been behind a bar before I came to work at the Coyote Ugly Saloon. Lil trained me herself. She didn't overload me with information at first. She didn't try to teach me how to mix drinks or even how to use the cash register. Basically I just followed her around and tried to absorb everything I could. I was obviously clueless. Not only could I not tend bar but I'd also shown up on my first night ridiculously dressed in tidy slacks and a button-down charcoal-gray wool sweater. During that first shift, my new boss gave me just two specific instructions about bartending. One: "Get those drinks out, and get them fast." Two: "Don't wear so much next time."

After a few months, these were my regulars: Redneck Lou, Bud Lite Lou, Chino, Gino, Anders, Morris, Reuben, Herbert (and his dog, Hoover), "Many Faces of Eve" Janet, the Plant Man, the Deaf Guy, Little Vinnie, Big Daddy, Beer Truck, Nazi Dave, Vietnam Bob, Spit-Take Phil, Eed-lee the Plumber, Bruce the Carpenter, Bill the Photographer, Ashley the Junkie, Slav the Pool Player, assorted employees of the Collins Bros. moving company, and virtually the entire glaziers' union. I have always hoped that Nazi Dave's nickname was an ironic joke.

Lil hired and fired many bartenders in her constant search for the perfect Coyote Ugly Saloon staff. Of course, she hired only women. Since most bar patrons were men, this was a great gimmick. I'll never understand why it's not a more common practice.

It was not always obvious what Lil was looking for in her women or why she was dissatisfied with those she discarded. She was ruthless. She gave no explanations. There were many bartenders at the Coyote Ugly Saloon whose careers lasted a single night. This could be perplexing. Many of the women that Lil fired were not only attractive but also perfectly competent bartenders. (Better than me, for instance, since they may have had previous experience at real bars, where one would be expected to know how to make a woo woo, a mud slide, or a grasshopper.) But there could be one thing about the girl that Lil didn't like, and that would be it—out the swingin' door.

There were bartenders who seemed to get fired because they were too fragile or too shy or too polite, of all things. (Early in my own Coyote Ugly Saloon career, I made the mistake of saying to a customer, "Here's your beer, sir." Lil overheard and shouted, "Don't ever call anyone in this place 'sir'!" So I said, "I'm terribly sorry. I meant to say, 'Here's your beer, douche bag.'" Lil and the customer laughed. And I thought, *Oh, I get it*, but I am a very quick study.) Some bartenders were gorgeous but not sexy, so what's the point? Some bartenders laughed a lot but were not funny themselves, so that didn't work either.

It all sounds ridiculously capricious, but Lil had a good eye. And what did she look for in us? Ultimately, Lil loved us only if you loved us. Because if you come to a bar called the Coyote Ugly Saloon and you order a Pabst Blue Ribbon beer and a shot of Old Weller, then you are seeking a very specific experience. You are probably looking for a bar something like the bar I visited once in Corona, New Mexico, with the sign on the door that read, PLEASE LEAVE ALL GUNS AND KNIVES IN YOUR CAR. THANK YOU KINDLY.

I myself was saved by Redneck Lou. Redneck Lou—the huge tattooed South Carolinian collector of Confederate-flag belt buckles—was one of Lil's best friends and the bar's consummate regular. He owned a denim jacket with an American flag on the back and a slogan underneath that read, TRY BURNING THIS ONE, ASSHOLE. Redneck Lou came into the bar during one of my early shifts, and we sang a Johnny Cash song together. I told him it was my favorite. Well, it was Redneck Lou's favorite too. He reported later to Lil, "I love that new bartender." That was it. I was in.

But I was never really sure how long I could stay in. As a Coyote Ugly Saloon bartender, I was to lure people into that place, keep them there as long as I could, and make damn sure they came back the next week. Our jobs depended upon this, and Lil never let her bartenders forget that.

No excuses were accepted. It didn't matter if it was a Sunday night or the weather was miserable or the New York Giants were in the Super Bowl. The bartender was responsible for bringing customers in. Period. Lil could do it. Lil could get crowds in that bar, and they'd never leave. If they started thinking about leaving, she would start feeding them free shots. She would press them to put their favorite songs on the jukebox. She would mercilessly tease them in front of their friends for being wimps. Whatever it took. Lil was expert at making patrons realize that while they may have *needed* to leave the bar, they didn't actually *want* to. People who thought they were on their way out found themselves, instead, suddenly buying a round for the whole bar.

Lil could pack that place during a Christmas-night blizzard, and she believed that any decent Coyote Ugly bartender should be able to do the same. That was only fair. She could also outdrink every single customer in the crowd. She believed any decent Coyote Ugly bartender should be able to do that too.

I was pretty good at filling the bar, but I couldn't drink on Lil's level. I could not toss back Kentucky bourbon for eight consecutive hours and still articulate English. Much less count change. So I invented a little trick (made public here for the first time) to save my life. I would pour a shot for the customer. I would pour a shot for myself. I kept a mug of Coke beside me at all times. The customer would swig, and I would swig. But I would not swallow. I would pretend to chase my shot with a slug of Coke, and then I would secretly spit the shot back into the Coke. Nobody ever knew.

Okay, some people knew. Bud Lite Lou knew. Bud Lite Lou was one of the few Coyote regulars sober enough to notice my ruse. Which he found amusing. He would beg me to sell him the mug full of whiskey, spit, and Coke at the end of the night. "I'll give you five bucks for it," he'd say.

But it didn't matter whether it was actual drinking or just the appearance of drinking. It honestly didn't matter. We were expected to be a little bit larger than life, or to pretend to be, or—at the very least—to want to be. We were the good-time girls. We were a cross between Old West dance hall hookers and gangsters' gun molls. Crack that gum, swing that ass, drink that shot, keep that change. If I didn't know you, I called you Mack, Jack, Slim, Dutch, Duke, Pal, or Buddy. You talked trash to me; I talked it right back but faster. Anything you needed, I set you up. You brought your friends in, I treated 'em right. You gave me trouble, I'd tell ya to scram. It was the 1990s, but talking like Mae West always helped.

There are so many secrets to getting a man to fall in love with his bartender, and so few of them have to do with mixing good drinks. At the very simplest level, the game goes like this: One afternoon you visit a bar. I am your bartender. You have two bottles of Miller, and you tell me about your upcoming divorce. I sympathize. I tell you a few lawyer jokes ("How do you keep a lawyer from drowning? Take your foot off his head."), and that cheers you up a bit. Three weeks later, you come into the bar again. This time you've brought your drinking buddies. As you enter, I say something like, "Hide your girlfriends—it's Jerry!" Then I say to your friends, "You know this maniac?" I open up a nice, cold bottle of Miller just for you, before you even sit down. Your friends are beginning to think that you are a very notorious individual indeed. You may even be wondering if I've mistaken you for some other Jerry. But you like the attention, so we continue the banter until your friends finally get up to play darts.

Then I lean over the bar, and I say very quietly, very gently, "How'd the court date go, Jer?"

You, Jerry, are now in love with me.

Or I could cut out the sympathetic-ear routine and just be a quick wit. There are men who love that too. If you were sitting at the bar when I cut into somebody else—somebody who really had it coming—you might fall in love with me just for that.

There was a man who used to come into the bar and regularly hassle me. He liked to say that I was too good for the place and managed to make this statement seem incredibly insulting. He had fun trying to guess what I really wanted to be in life or what career I had failed at so miserably that I was "only" a bartender. His name was Johnny.

"What are you doing working behind a bar, anyhow?" Johnny shouted.

"I like it here," I said. "I like being around sweethearts like you."

"I bet you want to be a movie star in real life."

"I want to be a scientist," I lied.

"A scientist?" Johnny repeated. He winked and said, "Maybe you should do some experiments with me, baby."

And then I said, "Looks like somebody already did, pal."

See how it works? My lines didn't have to be perfect. They just had to be quick. The regulars loved little scenes like this. They'd cheer me on. On another night, a well-dressed man walked into Coyote. He took a seat. He asked me, "What's up?"

I replied, "It's a preposition."

The regulars laughed. The well-dressed man shouted, "You're funny! I love you! If I had a car service pick us up right now and take us to JFK, would you go away with me tonight?"

"Nope," I said.

"Name your favorite city, anywhere in the world. I'll take you there right now."

"Minsk," I said.

"You're a riot!" he shouted. "I love you! At least let me take you out for dinner."

"Nope," I said.

Then the well-dressed man climbed up onto the bar. He knelt in beer puddles. He shouted, "I love this woman! I am publicly humiliating myself for her! Come to dinner with me!"

"Nope," I said.

"Look at that!" he shouted to the other customers. "She's hilarious! I love her!"

"If you stuck a knife into that guy right now," one of my regulars told me, "I'd deny that I ever saw a thing."

And all the other regulars laughed.

I had regulars who would come in and apologize to me for having missed my earlier shifts that week. Such a regular might say, "Remember me? You told me to come back and see you on Tuesday? I honestly meant to, but an emergency came up with my family. I'm so sorry. It won't happen again."

I had a lonely regular who used to say, "My cat keeps asking me when I'm finally going to bring you home to meet him. He's tired of me talking about you all the time."

I still have a lovely note that a very young regular gave me at the end of one shift. It reads, "If you can be so sweet and give me a call if you are not busy? To go out to dinner or to dancing, both!" The note is signed, "My name is Luis." A pin is attached that says PUERTO RICO.

There was a time, when I was a novice Coyote Ugly Saloon bartender, when I measured a good night by the number of marriage proposals I had received. I had a particularly determined regular who would ask me to marry him literally every time I walked past. For hours on end, we'd have this same conversation.

"Will you marry me, Liz?"

"Nope."

"Okay," he'd say.

Then the next bartender would arrive for the second shift.

"Will you marry me, Molly?" he'd ask.

I began regarding the words "Will you marry me?" as one of those phrases like "You got a staring problem, asshole?" or "I want to sing a song" or "I used to be a hell of a good-looking guy!"

It was obviously one of those things men say only when they are really, really drunk.

It is a great thing to be a much-loved bartender. It is a great thing to be a celebrity, even within a community of boxers. I found all that drunken love to be completely narcotic. A British friend came to New York to visit, and he watched me tend bar for hours. He said, "They all adore you. And they're all so miserable and pathetic. You, my dear, are the Queen of the Gutter!"

Fuck it, I love that title. I loved that gutter.

I loved "Many Faces of Eve" Janet, who was an attractive schizophrenic woman from the neighborhood. I would let Janet drink until she had a mood swing and started spitting at people, and then I would ask her to leave. Sometimes she left violently, but not always. "I'll tell you something, missy," Janet once said with great dignity as she was exiting. "If I had known how difficult you were going to be to manage,

I never would have accepted the job of being your guardian angel."

I loved Little Vinnie. Little Vinnie was an old man who showed up in the early afternoons. He drank White Russians with a straw as if he were drinking milk shakes at a soda shop. Little Vinnie was Ashley the Junkie's boyfriend (or perhaps her pimp). Ashley was not old, but she was worn and scrawny. She used to fall asleep at the bar and knock over her Long Island iced teas. (A Long Island iced tea is a wonder to make: Pour equal measures of all clear liquors—vodka, gin, rum, tequila, triple sec—into a pint glass over ice. Add a splash of Coke. Serve. Ashley the Junkie could drink four of these gravediggers in an hour.)

I loved Ashley, and she loved me. She had a fantasy that someday the two of us would visit Great Adventure Theme Park together.

"We'll go in a convertible," she'd say. "We'll sure get the guys, won't we? I mean, look at us—blond, thin . . ."

Here she would trail off. Here Ashley the Junkie would run out of similarities between us.

"That sounds like fun, Ashley," I'd say. "Let's do that soon."

As for Little Vinnie, he was the worst conversationalist in history. All he wanted to do was shake my hand and say, "How ya doin'?" whenever I brought him another White Russian. Other than that, forget it. Eventually, I realized that he was almost entirely deaf. If Vinnie couldn't hear me, he'd get frustrated and assume that I was insulting him. He'd burst out, "Aw, shut the hell up! Just shut the hell up and leave me alone!"

Some quiet afternoons, it would just be the three of us in that bar for hours. Ashley the Junkie, Little Vinnie, and me. Ashley would eventually fall asleep and knock over her Long Island iced tea. I would clean it up so she wouldn't get it in her hair. I would keep bringing Little Vinnie his White Russians, and he would shake my hand and grin happily every time.

"How ya doin'?"

"Doing great, Vinnie," I'd always say. "I'm doing real good."

There were people who said that the Coyote Ugly Saloon was a dump full of losers, but the words *dump* and *loser* are, after all, relative. At the time, for instance, I was subletting a drug addict's apartment, just off Avenue B. When I moved in, there was nothing in the refrigerator but a syringe, and the microwave literally contained a layer of topsoil. I had to take care of the drug addict's three hideous cats, which were about as domesticated as weasels. The whole building smelled like a slaughterhouse. A visiting friend said sympathetically, "Even Henry Miller never stayed in a place this gross." Compared with my home, the Coyote Ugly Saloon was a cathedral.

And as far as losers go, I'd just had my heart broken myself. Everyone has his heartbreak story (and I've heard them all), so I'll keep mine simple: I loved someone, and he moved away. I was inestimably sad. Like a newborn, I would cry myself to sleep and wake up in the middle of the night to cry some more. Who was I to talk about losers? I was happy only when I was swimming long laps at the pool or tending bar at the Coyote Ugly Saloon.

And after a few weeks at the Coyote Ugly, I quit swimming.

Every bar is a monument to talk, which is why very lonely people and very gregarious people need bars. As a bar customer, you can engage in only two conversations, one to your left and one to your right. But as a bartender, I could engage in fourteen conversations at once. I wasn't the prettiest bartender at the Coyote Ugly Saloon, but I was damn sure the best talker. I could bandy with any man and banter with his brother. I was completely awake during that year, especially during the long night shifts. I wasn't the belle of the ball; I was the bouncing ball. You all looked to me.

By one in the morning on a typical night, for example, I'm already up on the bar, dancing to an Allman Brothers song on the jukebox. The brothers are singing, "Sometimes I feel like I been tied to the whipping post." I tear off my belt and whip the bar to the beat. Then I whip Redneck Lou (who always volunteers), and I do it in such an ironic way that you, the customer, die laughing.

By two in the morning, I have Reuben on top of the bar with me. He's wearing a Zorro mask I made by ripping off a piece of his T-shirt. He's wearing a cape I made out of a plastic Budweiser banner. I give him one garbage-can lid, and I take another. We hold them like shields. We have broomsticks, and we begin to sword-fight. He shouts, "Die! Die!" People come off the street to watch and then stay to drink.

By three in the morning, Spit-Take Phil has found a latex glove and filled it with beer. He pokes holes in the glove's fingers and climbs onto the bar. He gets on all fours and tucks the bloated glove into his belt, so it hangs like an udder. He moos. Naturally, I grab two rubber bands and quickly put my hair in farm-girl pigtails. And then I milk him. The crowd is cheering.

By four in the morning, I start threatening to close. By five I actually start the slow process of throwing everybody out. "Last call!" I say. "Last call for alcohol!"

By six in the morning, I am standing on the bar again. I have turned all the lights on brightly; the jukebox is off. But you, the devoted customers, still won't leave.

"It's motel time," I drone. "I don't care what you do. Just don't do it here."

But you still stay, planted on your bar stools. So I grab a broom, and I step onto the bar with it. I start sweeping your drinks off the bar, with a light little flick and a fake Cinderella smile. The place is a mess anyhow. The bottles roll to the floor and break; the beer spills everywhere. It doesn't matter. It really makes no difference at all.

"*Tra-la-la!*" I sing. "Please go home now!"

Finally you leave. Before I lock up for the night, I set off a roach bomb in the middle of the floor strong enough to kill a mule train, and then I run out the door before the chemicals hit. Outside the sun has not yet come up, but the sky has a magnificent breaking light. The only cars on First Avenue are the garbage trucks and the newspaper delivery vans. (One particular morning, I rounded the corner at Ninth Street and found Tom, the owner of the Village Idiot, draped over a mailbox, snoring. He was drunk and sleeping, with his cheek pressed lovingly against the cool, blue cheek of the United States Postal Service. "Good night, Tommy," I said.)

Back at my apartment, I pull a wad of money from my jeans. My tips. A thick stack of bills, folded like a fat taco. I peel off whatever I am wearing and then face the biggest dilemma of the night: Do I throw my clothes in the laundry? Or just throw them away?

At the Coyote Ugly Saloon, we used to say, "Every good joke begins, 'A man walks into a bar . . .'"

"You don't have much respect for men, do you?" my brother-in-law asked me at the time of my bartending career. "You're beginning to think we're jokes, aren't you?"

Not true. Not at all true. For instance, a man walked into a bar one night, and two and a half years later, I married him. I met him at the Coyote Ugly Saloon, and it was later at the Coyote Ugly Saloon that he asked me, "Would you marry a man who asked you to marry him after he'd had a few drinks?"

"If I married every man who asked me after a few drinks," I said, "I would have been gone long ago."

But I married him anyway. An easy choice, because he was the nicest one. People think it's an odd way to meet a husband and an odd way to be proposed to, but it makes perfect sense to me. I have always loved a good bar. I come from a family of good drinkers. There was one year when my dad was making his own beer, my sister was writing a three-hundred-page doctoral dissertation about women's drinking during Prohibition, my mother was counseling teenage alcoholics, and I was bartending. As a family, we orbited the universe of inebriation. Back when I was seven years old, my grandfather sat me and my sister on his knee and told us, wisely, "Whenever you're in a strange bar and you don't know the bartender, always order a martini. It's pure alcohol, so he can't stiff you on the booze."

When I was eight years old, that same grandfather took me on a tour of the Matt brewery in Utica, New York. At the end of the tour, the guides led us into a dark turn-of-the-century tavern. The adults each got a free sample of Matt draft beer. I was hoisted up onto a bar stool. The bartender slid me over a frosty root beer in a frozen mug, along with a basket of pretzels. The sweet-and-salt taste of that combination was extraordinary. The tavern was carved from dark woods and decorated with a great, smoky mirror. Decadent red velvet drapes kept the sun out. My fingers left prints in the frost on my glass. The low laughter of that tavern is still the most adult sound I can remember.

I planted my elbows on the bar in exactly the manner of my grandfather. I was settling in. I was the prettiest girl in the whole bar.

CITY OF TONGUES

Jenna Wortham

Most people in New York have a half-life, an expiration date, an unknown period of time before they will say enough is enough, a moment they will concede to the city's toughness, its cruelty and hardness, and start saying their unsentimental goodbyes.

For my mom, it was about an hour after she arrived for her first visit. We got separated on a subway platform, pushed apart by post-work people unloading off a train, all tired bodies wrapped in puffer coats and weighed down by grocery bags. I spotted her first and called her name, but she didn't hear me. I could see her twisting this way and that, trying to find me, the panic rising in her eyes. It was the last time she would make the trip.

For my ex-boyfriend, it was about a year. After living in San Francisco for a few years, I was offered a job in New York and so we went. We arrived in the dead of November. We didn't have the right shoes or warm-enough coats and we spent our nights huddled in a drafty apartment eating delivery and watching Netflix on the couch. It wasn't the life either of us had pictured, but I was convinced the city would soon reveal its charms. He couldn't wait for it; he packed up his things and our cat. She didn't like New York either. She refused to drink the cloudy water that dribbled from our faucet, sniffing it a few times before looking at me unhappily and skulking into the bedroom. After they left, I cried for weeks, but eventually, surprisingly, relief bloomed in my bones, replacing the inconsolable desperation that had settled in there before. It felt like, Now I can start living my life in New York.

When someone is done with the city, they don't have to tell you. You can read it in their eyes, their shoulders, and the slow, shuffle-y way that they walk. They aren't trying to keep up with anyone or anything anymore.

I saw my friend Jay's moment unfold before my eyes. It came in the middle of that interminable winter, those endless months of freezing wind, piles of slush and cold slices of air on tender, sun-starved flesh. No one could register anything on their faces and limbs but the bitterness of the weather. It pressed us all into defeat. Sometimes people didn't even register that any other humans were alive. They crashed into your body and stepped on your feet in a hurry to get out of the cold. But who could blame them?

I met Jay on my first adult visit to New York and Brooklyn. I'd come before as a kid, with my sixth-grade class. We rode the ferry to Ellis Island and saw where the people arrived and underwent inspection to see if they were fit to enter the country. On the way back to Manhattan, I leaned my face over the side of the boat, watching the lines it cut through the water and feeling the spray streaking salt on my cheeks. My glasses slid down my nose and off my face so fast it didn't even register until they disappeared out of sight and into the river. For the rest of the trip, I couldn't see anything, just smears of blurry lights and rain-bright streets. When I got back home to Virginia, my mother asked me how I liked the city. I told her it was beautiful.

When I came back a decade later, I was in town to visit my best friend and former roommate from college. She was living in Greenpoint with her boyfriend, a film guy named Jay who wore a weathered leather jacket, took us to noisy concerts and small art shows, and bought us shots of Jameson watered down with ice. He was fifteen, maybe twenty years older than we were. The first Sunday I was in town, he woke up early and ran out to get meatball subs from an Italian place nearby and bounced on the balls of his feet while I bit into the soft bread and seasoned, tomatoey meat. He gallantly traded sandwiches with me after I found a bit of bone in mine. He was a good guy. I came to love New York quick and hard, like a new crush, and it was mostly because of the way Jay loved New York and the way he showed us how to live in it.

Even then, the city was speaking to me; I just didn't know how to respond yet. I didn't even know the city had a language, its own form of nonverbal communication that let you know whether you were in the right place at the right time. There were so many distractions to keep you from noticing—the heat, the cold, the bad smells, the good smells, the rodents, the piles of garbage and the inescapable presence of people, everywhere—it's not surprising that it's hard to find the calm, the beauty, the enjoyable mired in all of it. But the city was remarkable at making up for itself. I remember once hugging a friend outside a subway entrance, both of us woozy with booze and just holding each other, hard, and happy, before pulling apart to see Cuba Gooding Jr. standing about a foot away, swaying and grinning in our direction. We all burst out laughing before going our separate ways. The high from moments like that could last for weeks, maybe months, lifting you up over the grossness of everything else, and in New York, those moments are never in short supply. Getting up at dawn to go to the Rockaways on summer weekends was one of the first secret pleasures that I discovered here, the way the subway could transport you somewhere so wholly different, full of surfers and hot dogs and moms dunking their babies in warm, frothy water. It was so absurdly different from the city landscape that it was practically perfect. Once, on a too-hot summer night, we jumped from a dock into Jamaica Bay in Queens, as glittering planes lifted off overhead. Our splashing activated the bioluminescent bacteria that lived in the water, which groggily came to life, streaking the water with glowing patches of blue-green light.

Living in New York felt like I was back in school learning to read and do math all over again, and not just in the memorization of all the subway lines and street signs so I could navigate the streets and stations with the deliberate movements of a local. Quickly sizing someone or a situation up became crucial for social interactions and for avoiding embarrassment, like understanding the intention of the person beside you at the bar or quickly (and accurately) coming to the conclusion that the reason people were acting strangely about the person you were talking to who looked vaguely famous was in fact that they *were* someone famous.

The calculus and physics of knowing where to walk and at which exact moment to avoid clipping strangers came first, although not easily. I remember clotheslining a little boy on a sidewalk in the West Village with the strap of my purse. It looped around his neck and yanked him off his Razor scooter. I whirled around and knelt down to see if he was okay. "Oh, he's fine," his mother said, tugging him up and along.

My first few months in New York, I couldn't figure out how to walk through the turnstiles that line some of the exits from the subway stations. Not the smaller, waist-high ones; those are idiot-proof. The full-height ones. Those are six or seven feet tall and installed to prevent people from jumping over to avoid paying the fare. I understood how they worked, as a concept, but every time I lined up to walk through, I would watch the person ahead of me enter the steel trap, panic, and then hustle myself in behind them, two bodies pressed into a space designed for one medium-sized person. The second or third time it happened, I shuffle-apologized myself through the turn with a woman who threw me the most exaggerated look over her should that simply said, *Girl.*

I would hear that voice in my head again and again over the first few years I lived in New York. One time the lurch of the train tossed me into the lap of a petite woman who was reading a book. I laughed and apologized. She was not amused. Again, there was that look. *Girl.* It came again and again and not necessarily from women. When I stopped too abruptly on the street or changed direction, disrupting the flow of the people moving around me, or didn't have my credit card at the ready at the deli or couldn't find my ID to show a bouncer at a bar. That look, it was always the same. *Girl.*

Cataloging New York's taxonomy of sounds and smells came later, like knowing immediately why one car on the subway was emptied of passengers when the others were at capacity. Learning to discern between types of screams—which tenors meant playful and which ones meant horror—took longer, but the skill would almost always be the most useful. The art of ignoring took longer to perfect; I wasn't used to the dead-eyed stare you give when you don't want to be bothered or something weird is going down and you don't want to be involved.

I didn't understand it until it happened to me, until I was causing the crazy on a sunny afternoon in the East Village. I stood under a tree on First Avenue, sobbing, mouth open wide but silent. I was on the phone with my dying father, who had called to tell me about his day. But he couldn't get through a sentence; he struggled to catch his breath, and as I stood on the street, listening to his ragged, painful attempts to inhale, the hordes of fresh young bodies talking, half running, enjoying the day punched me in my chest until I was crying, half hunched over, facing the street. I couldn't move or figure out where to go, but people parted respectfully, peacefully, giving me a shadow of space in a city that has so little. One stranger paused behind me and briefly rested a hand on my back before quickly moving on down the street. It felt full of compassion and recognition without any obligation or acknowledgment required in return and I welcomed it.

Months—or maybe years—later I was waiting for a train, silently making a list of the errands I planned to run that day, when a woman started screaming. The pitch sang of pure pain. My eyes focused and I saw a young girl wailing and holding her mouth. She had somehow gotten injured while getting off the train. She fast-walked toward me; I could see the water welling in her eyes.

"What just happened?" she moaned. When she opened her mouth to talk, I could see that her teeth were red with blood and her lip was rapidly swelling in size.

I confessed I didn't know, that I hadn't been paying attention. "But you were right there," she shrieked, taking a step toward me.

"I know," I replied. "But I didn't see what happened," I said, moving away. There were no limits to the sudden acts of cruelty that erupted in the city, often without warning or explanation.

But even with that, even then, the feeling that anything is possible, that anything could happen at any given moment, thrilled me. It probably should have terrified me, and certainly some things did: the disappearance of a sweet boy named Avonte Oquendo, followed by the discovery of his dismembered remains; living below crazy alcoholics who beat each other in a stairwell and called me the n-word when I threatened to call the cops; picking up the pieces of the city in the aftermath of Hurricane Sandy. Sometimes, the horrors of city life that seemed too terrible to be endured became manageable once you realized they were universal experiences. Hearing that other people had dealt with mouse infestation or felt the furry scurry of a rat over their sandal-clad foot made those quiet horrors much more bearable and, at times, felt like hallmarks of a true, authentic New Yorker, who could deal with those things and emerge unscathed.

But beyond all that, there was still a sort of sweetness, at least for me. Things like passing a bottle of ice-cold champagne among four friends as we raced down the frigid and near-empty streets of the Lower East Side one night right after New Year's, or getting the exact same thing from the same Midtown food cart so many times that the vendors started having my coffee ready the moment they spotted me heading their way. Seeing people give money to buskers and the homeless and then, later, keeping a little extra change in your pocket so you could do it yourself. Watching a sunset on a roof somewhere and seeing the whole mess of the city in all of its entire broken and glorious splendor. Having someone knock into you and apologize in such a kind and genuine way that you start doing it yourself, tossing quick little "sorrys" when you accidentally cut off or brush into someone and become amazed at how different the city becomes as a result of that one small thing. My favorite thing in New York is the way people who live here give and ask each other for directions on a daily basis. It's the purest transaction, one that never asks for anything but a quick and honest reply. People who stick their heads in a train and ask where it goes almost always get an answer that doesn't expect a reward; it's an incredible thing to witness and is better than some of the forced politeness of the West Coast and other places that I've lived.

In the beginning, New York always felt like the set of a movie. I shared a cab with a cute-enough guy who asked me for a date instead of my half of the fare. He took me to a steamy oyster bar and told me his favorite thing in the city was the choreography of people moving about in Grand Central Station. He smiled dopily at me and swayed his hands around in his imitation of a symphony conductor while I tried to keep the expression on my face in neutral. But then, once, I was passing through Grand Central Station after a meeting and saw the matrix of people dotting that beautiful marble floor and saw what he meant, for a brief moment.

There are some universal truths that possess people living in New

York, making them swear by a certain restaurant's dish, certain art or film openings, extravagant bars of locally made chocolate or bath soap, the view of the city from this rooftop or that, a karaoke night at some out-of-the-way sailor bar. But these phases are more than temporary trends, they're a way of making life in the city more livable— and often lovable—by carving off the best pieces of city living and presenting them to others to sample and enjoy, as a way of balancing out craziness and the hardness that can occupy too much of our time.

In the 1994 romantic comedy *It Could Happen to You*, Nicolas Cage's character, a police officer, gives Bridget Fonda's character, a waitress, half of his lottery winnings as a tip. The entire city falls in love with their story. It appears all over the local papers and there's even a moment in a hotel where two bellhops exclaim that they've run into the cop and the waitress. I remember hating that part in the movie, thinking that there was no way that an entire city could be so captivated by their story that they would be recognizable on the street.

But of course they would be and of course we would know them— this city loves a good story, inexhaustible tidbits of small talk that coffee-cart guys tell their regulars and that people gossip about at dinner parties and work. These were the things I wanted to explain to Jay when I saw him on the train, when he looked at me out of the corner of his eye and said that he was leaving for good. This would be his last year in New York, which was, by then, my fifth.

I wanted to remind him about catching a glimpse of the sky at sunset, infused with soft blues and blazing oranges, remind him about nights that took a wild surprise turn and left you exhilarated and reinvigorated about the promises of love and life and the meaning of it all. I wanted to tell him that maybe he'd just forgotten how to speak city and that maybe it would come back. But he just chewed his lip and shook his head and got off at the next stop and I got off at mine.

BUT WHY DID YOU MOVE HERE?

Stephen Elliott

When I came to New York it was 1994 and I was twenty-two. I didn't know anybody or anything, and I stayed in the hostel on 125th in Harlem. I was just passing through, which was a habit of mine for a few years. What I remember were the cheap bagel sandwiches they sold at every bodega (and that the bodegas were open twenty-four hours a day, thousands of them, all with garish yellow and orange signs). The sandwiches were only two or three dollars, giant piles of turkey with mustard, always cut in half, enough for two meals. I was totally alone and I like to think that we all go through periods like that.

A year later, following the best summer of my life, I overdosed on heroin in the attic of a rooming house in Evanston. I'm not sure how that fits in this story but it changed everything in me. In fact, I remember my friend Louie visiting the hospital where I was interned for eight days unable to walk and he said, "You better never write about this." And I think I made a joke or smiled and shook my head and then asked him to leave. I spent the rest of my twenties in Seattle and Los Angeles and Chicago and at a ski resort in Colorado. I ran out of gas on the Oakland Bay Bridge on my way into San Francisco and that's where I ended up for most of fifteen years.

When I was thirty I published two books with a small press that has since gone bankrupt. There were a few short trips to New York, book related, between Midtown hotels decorated with *New Yorker* cartoons and the Javits Center, where I saw firsthand the size of a banner a larger publishing house might purchase and display for an author they really believed in.

In 2004 I was fanatically political the way some people watch football with their whole body painted green in the freezing cold. Or the way we followed Michael Jordan in Chicago when the city shut down and there were no cars on the street and you couldn't hear anything anywhere except Red Kerr announcing the game.

Monitoring the political scores soaked up all my time and anxiety then. Howard Dean was in Vermont, John Kerry was in Boston, Richard Gephardt was in Iowa (not that it mattered), and New York City was on the train or bus, or occasionally car if I was hitchhiking between these places and Washington, DC.

I had a friend who lived in Williamsburg and another who lived in Park Slope, but that's an entirely different story. My friend had come to New York to be where things were "happening." Later he got married and had a child and moved back to San Francisco, where years later, during a rolling blackout, I thought I noticed him bent over a table full of cocaine. But in 2004 he opened his apartment to me until his roommate could no longer stand it and changed the lock on the doors, at least emotionally.

It was during that election that I started to recognize something in New York. The diversity for one thing. Millionaires were riding subways with homeless people. Also the ambition, similar to the ambition in Los Angeles but more palatable. In New York people wanted to make it as something. As a fashion designer, as a writer, as an artist. In Los Angeles it seemed people just wanted to make it. They wanted their name in the credits and didn't care if they worked on the movie or not.

There are two kinds of artists in Los Angeles, players and suckers. The suckers were the ones trying to make something good.

Now I think what I was starting to notice was my own ambition. That year was full of hope right until the day after the election, when I wandered into the ocean in South Florida and got sick for a long time.

In mid-2005 I decided to make the move from San Francisco to New York and sublet my apartment. Then, two weeks before I was supposed to go, I fell in love with someone I met online and called the sublet off. The next two years disappeared on the West Coast and in the curves of her waist and sound of her voice. When I try to remember what happened, I see a small brightly lit room and I'm alone in it in a kind of haze wondering what happened to all my friends. Or I imagine falling asleep in a cage and waking up with a blanket, the door unlocked.

When it was over I surveyed the wreckage. I'd lost my job teaching writing at the university. I still wanted to go to New York but a murder trial (not mine, but one I was somehow intimately connected to) ate up the next two years. And then in 2010 I finally made it to New York. But something was still wrong. One day in the park I started crying. The next day I cried as well. Manhattan had shifted to Brooklyn but it seemed like that was happening all over America, except maybe Baltimore, Detroit, and everywhere that wasn't a large city. The disappearing middle class and resulting stratification and spiraling rents. After a month of crying I went to see a psychiatrist in the East Village and she tried to have me committed but I ran off and wasn't around when the police arrived looking for me. I had to go back to California for a while.

San Francisco was like that "ideal" girl with flaxen hair and perfect skin, the kind of girl I'd never been attracted to. I had health insurance in San Francisco that wouldn't transfer and I got diagnosed with something fairly serious. In fact, when I was diagnosed I thought my life was like a merry-go-round and the ride had stopped and I had to get off.

I had a girlfriend and she would tie me up and dress me in women's clothes. She loved me but was unhappy with my seeming inability to love her back. I did love her, I thought, but not passionately. And I thought there was nothing wrong with my love for her; it was love without all the destructive irrational emotions. I had a cheap apartment, an office space for a magazine I'd started, a network of good friends, and San Francisco, a hard city to move to, had become easy.

The air in San Francisco is clean and cold but never that cold. San Francisco is like a place where you can sit at a counter and order a slice of pie and stare down into a bay surrounded by mountains and then the Golden Gate Bridge, tankers floating on the ocean like tiny birds. Sometimes in San Francisco, when I was teaching test preparation for law school candidates, I would wake up in a small apartment in Chinatown and walk down the hill toward the Embarcadero, buttoning my shirt, shocked that I was alive for this beauty.

And I was in love with a woman in Oakland who hadn't spoken to me in years but I still thought about her all the time. It was the most ridiculous love story ever told. She wanted to take pictures with me for her website. And then she wanted to take more pictures. Eventually we were having sex while her ex-boyfriend was photographing us and I didn't even know he was there. I loved her the way my girlfriend wanted me to love her. I wanted to inhale her. When I stroked her shoulders it was like I was memorizing her body with my fingers. But she was monogamous, and as long as we were taking pictures it wasn't cheating, and then I pointed out that it was still cheating and that was that.

Somehow New York was like the woman I was in love with who didn't love me back. The thing is, she never said no. "No" would have changed everything. I've always taken no for an answer. Instead New York said maybe. Before she disappeared for good she would kiss me occasionally, stop by unannounced. When really desperate she might spread her legs for twenty blissful minutes. And then was on to someone else. She was impossible, which is a facet of the city. Talk to anyone in New York, they talk about sacrifices. They talk about the tiny apartment, the commute, the freezing winter and muggy summers. Then they say, "But I live in New York!" And they say it like it's obvious. All the things they give up to be here, well, who wouldn't?

By 2011 I'd discovered the Brooklyn and Manhattan Bridges, the carousel in Dumbo, been back and forth so many times I knew the intersections by number. I was so desperate to connect, like I'd had a ticket to the moon and missed the shuttle launch. When I talked about New York and San Francisco I said it was like being in love with two women. Except I wasn't in love with San Francisco anymore and I didn't want anyone to know. I never said goodbye to San Francisco. I was back and forth for a couple of years working on a movie, couch-surfing, transient, a foot on either coast.

And then the movie was wrapped and I thought, *What if I just didn't go back?*

They say every story is a love story or a story about loneliness. I don't think I've been in love too many times but how many times are you supposed to fall in love? And I've certainly never felt safe with someone I've truly loved. Not if I loved them intensely, the way my ex-girlfriend wanted me to. Not even if they woke up crying because they'd had a dream I was going to break up with them. Not even when they left their husband. Not even when I drove them home in a stolen car. Sometimes love isn't obvious. It's more like a subway rumbling beneath your ribs. Sometimes love is like a snow you're ready for. I used to say there was something in New York that made me feel alive. Those were the times I forgot the cable cars and that hill in Chinatown. I forgot the hundreds of people crowded into the Makeout Room for our monthly events. I forgot the Fort Mason Youth Hostel and the monuments to World War II, and Sausalito across the black water and the tufts of fog caught on the bridge and sitting back there late at night with a couple of sheets and a couple of beers. I forgot everything about San Francisco and when talking about New York I'd say, "It's like there's cocaine in the air." Maybe that doesn't sound like love to you, but I had an unusual childhood. And when the time finally came, which in fact it never did . . . It was never going to be obvious, or easy, or justifiable, and I jumped for no reason. Because I loved New York and everything about it.

Two years later my stuff is still in San Francisco, and I've signed a lease in Bed-Stuy. After years of screaming, I left San Francisco like a whisper. If anybody asked I made excuses, like the need for collaborators, the desire to work with great actors (and the actors in New York are, on balance, the best in the world). I'd say anything except the truth, which is I have no idea. Maybe I don't know how to love, or I love too strongly and then not at all, which is the same thing. Sometimes I say San Francisco isn't the city I arrived at, with its history of poetry. The place of the beatniks, the Summer of Love, *Rolling Stone*, Jefferson Starship, Hunter Thompson. The place Joan Didion wrote *Slouching Towards Bethlehem* and the Hells Angels knifed a fan at a free concert in the park. The focal point of the speed epidemic and third-wave feminism. Where the peace movement first turned violent. All of that was gone. I'd point to all the cranes on Market Street. This whole city is luxury condos, I'd spit. But at a certain age you know that's just bullshit. You know what you don't know. And if I was really pressured, if San Francisco cried and begged me to come back and wouldn't listen to any of my excuses, I would have to shrug my shoulders as if at a loss, and say not for the first time, "But I love her."

MANHATTAN

Julie Klam

My "when I was a kid we had to walk eight miles to school in the snow" story I tell my ten-year-old daughter is about how I lived before On Demand and DVDs . . . that in order to watch a movie you had to look through a newspaper and find out when it was on and then stay up for it and you had to pee during the commercials. At this point she needs a cold compress, but I've always believed in telling it like it is.

My family got our first VCR around 1983. I remember my dad telling us about when he first watched Jack Benny and it was a similar experience. The first three movies we rented were *Airplane!*, *Annie Hall*, and *Arthur*. (I assume the next ones were *Breakfast at Tiffany's*, *Bananas*, and *Breaking Away*, but I can't recall.) We rented them on a Monday so we could keep them for Free Tuesday and return them Wednesday. During those heady few days I watched and rewatched *Annie Hall* and *Arthur* (*Airplane!* was kind of a boy movie) over and over till late into the night (which would kind of become my "thing"). I know I thought they were good and funny, but I mostly remember that they took place in my favorite spot in the world, New York, New York. The city so nice, they named it twice.

I lived an hour north of "the city" as we called it, in Katonah, a nice little town, a village, if you will. My parents were from Manhattan and the Bronx and anxious to have their kids breathe fresh air and gambol in the grass and canter on horseback and stick their hands under a chicken and pull out an egg. Which of course was all great for everyone. Except me. I didn't really like "nature" or "to go outside." I wasn't nuts about the big, sprawling house either. Everything was a hike; from my bedroom to the kitchen was a good forty-minute walk. (Okay, maybe not, but you know how lazy kids are? It felt like it.)

It wasn't that I didn't want to go outside anywhere. I liked to be outdoors on Madison Avenue. The gummy pavement under my feet felt homey. My best days were going in to work with my dad and getting to play in his office and eat lunch at Kaplan's at the Delmonico or stay over at my aunt Mattie's across from Bloomingdale's and eat cheeseburgers and hot fudge sundaes and go to matinees. She and I saw *The Goodbye Girl* on Fifty-Seventh and Third at the now-defunct Sutton movie theater, and I thought no one was luckier than Quinn Cummings, who played the little girl in that movie. She got to live in Manhattan in a cool apartment with her mom and Richard Dreyfuss (*"I don't want the panties hanging on the rod!"*).

The fact was, in those early years I didn't get to go to the city all that often. Mostly I spent my days in Katonah dreaming of the time that I'd be a grown-up and sleep in the city that never did.

Whatever your personal opinion of Woody Allen is, and I know you've got one, he was instrumental in my falling in love with this town. I had a book of his screenplays that I got at Caldor's. The cover showed the iconic still photo from *Manhattan* with Woody and Diane Keaton sitting in the fading light before the Fifty-Ninth Street Bridge, rich, crisp black and white, of course, the way it was meant to be.

And it wasn't just the aching beauty, it was the life of *Manhattan*. Everyone was in therapy and ate out in restaurants and had apartments filled with fabulous art and overstuffed bookshelves and black soap, and through it all Gershwin played. The conversation was filled with witty bon mots and intellectual discourse and it was very cool to be "Jewy."

My sense was that if I lived in Manhattan, I would belong there. I wouldn't feel out of place or lonely or unathletic or scared. A close friend of my parents who was a beauty editor in the city told me she would *never* exercise because what if she broke a nail? Those were my people. However I was would be hip and okay. Manhattan wasn't for cheerleaders.

When I first moved there, I was appropriately at NYU film school, and though we weren't watching Woody Allen, we were living it. I walked around with my Walkman, listening to his soundtracks. It was then that I graduated to the grittier Martin Scorsese New York City movies, *Taxi Driver* and *Mean Streets*. And Lumet's *Dog Day Afternoon*. I could walk around Manhattan then and still see the stores and buildings that made up the sets for the New York City in films. It was the land of oddballs, misfits, beautiful (misunderstood) women, and guys who would punch people for them. I spent my after-school hours in revival movie houses that smelled like roach spray, where I watched the glamorous New York of the 1930s with the butlers and ladies in satin and feather gowns who swept into their sparkling apartments and fixed themselves a highball. I wanted to live in that Manhattan too, though I worried I might have ended up the Margaret Dumont character.

You know the difference between New York and LA? That's what every stand-up comic asked during the 1980s, and they all had their own not necessarily funny take on it. (Woody of course said Los Angeles's only cultural advantage was right on red.) But to me the difference was that New York was all together and Los Angeles was spread out. There are other differences too. Like whenever I go to LA, I am sure that I'm the fattest, palest, and oldest person there. (By the way, the irony that there are only two US cities worthy of comparison is not lost on me.) I went out there for a meeting in the early nineties and was staying at the Chateau Marmont. My meeting was a street away and when I asked the woman at the desk for directions, she told me this long, roundabout way to go—take a left up this hill over to Sunset . . . I said, "Isn't it like half a block away?" And she said, "Yeah, but blah blah is a one-way street." And I said, "But I'm walking." And someone shrieked and a dog fainted. I did walk too. I was like Ratso Rizzo to them.

But in New York . . . I could and would walk. I was interning on *Late Night with David Letterman*, and a friend, the head writer at the time, and I would walk from the Battery to the Upper West Side and just stop in any place that caught our fancy. Even when I'd take a train, it somehow felt very compact and the opposite of the sprawling town I grew up in, let alone my enormous dumb house. I liked that people lived close together: it seemed much more comprehensive. Like we were all in a doll house together. When I moved into my first "real" apartment, I was proud of the fact that from anyplace in my studio, you could see the whole rest of it. Not for hide-and-seekers, but cozy nonetheless.

The thing about the New York in movies and TV shows is they never tell you that though it's easy to get here, it's hard to stay. It's like being in love with this amazing person who is funny and breathtaking and constantly surprising. Who shows up late at night at your door with amazing trinkets from flea markets—things that seem to have fallen from the moon—and the most wonderful food you've ever eaten. But he's wearing a big coat and he keeps your money in the pockets, the pockets have big gaping holes in them, and the money just falls out. I've been here for thirty years now, I've been married here, had a baby and seven dogs, been mired in the public school *mishegos*, gotten divorced, and struggled a lot. I've been broke and then I've been at the place where I looked back at it and thought, Oh, I thought *that* was broke. Now *this* is *broke*.

And through it all my parents, my brothers, certain friends, my husband, even my die-hard New York aunt have said, "Move somewhere cheaper! Somewhere that is easier!" Did you know that you could have a whole house in a town you don't want to live in for five dollars? (Actually they pay you to live there!)

But New York is my home. And New Yorkers are my home. Even, or maybe especially, the crazy ones. I never feel out of place here except when I meet someone—usually the parent of a friend of my daughter's—who is talking about moving out. There are two kinds of New Yorkers, the ones who could never leave and the other ones. I don't look down on them, I just can't understand how they can do it. Believe me, I know I'm the nutty one. I used to start off every first date telling the guy I'd never leave New York. (That was right before I told him the style of engagement diamond I preferred.)

And I know it's probably true that life would be easier somewhere else. That New York Hollywood movies don't tell you how hard it is. I'd like to say I don't mind the hard, but I hate it. God, I wish it was easier. I wish I lived in Woody Allen's apartment (though I hear these days people scream at him whenever he goes outside). It doesn't really matter because I simply couldn't survive somewhere else. I've been here this long, I'm not giving up now.

And though there are times when I fantasize about leaving my apartment that's so small you have to go into the hall to change your mind, and moving to a wall-to-wall-carpeted split-level home in suburbia, and getting in my car and driving to a supermarket and putting my groceries in my trunk and driving back home into my two-car garage with the big washer and dryer and storage for reams of paper towels, there are still a million times a day that I see something here that I wouldn't see anywhere else (follow me on Instagram and you'll know this is true) and I wouldn't trade it.

Toward the end of *Manhattan,* there's that scene of Woody Allen lying on the couch talking into a tape recorder about what makes life worth living. It's Woody's list: Groucho Marx, Willie Mays, the second movement of the *Jupiter Symphony,* Louie Armstrong's recording of "Potato Head Blues," Swedish movies, *Sentimental Education* by Flaubert, Marlon Brando, Frank Sinatra, those incredible apples and pears by Cézanne, the crabs at Sam Wo's. I can honestly say that not a single one of those items is on my list. In fact, my list is very short. My kid, my dogs, and this beautiful, fucked-up, heartbreaking mother of a city.

ROYALTY

Susan Orlean

My first apartment in Manhattan was on West End Avenue near Seventy-second Street or, as I soon came to think of it, about two blocks from Gray's Papaya, which is at Broadway and Seventy-second. My husband's office was around the corner from Papaya Kingdom, which was at Broadway and Fiftieth. My gym was down the street from Papaya King, which was on Eighty-sixth between Second and Third. My best friend lived near Papaya Prince, in the West Village. I spent a lot of my afternoons at the Mid-Manhattan branch of the public library, a few blocks from Papaya World. I can't remember exactly where Papaya Princess was, but I know I passed it now and then, in cabs. Before I moved to New York, twenty-eight years ago, I hadn't had much contact with papayas. I knew they existed, and I saw them occasionally in supermarkets—stickered with their country of origin, like luggage—but they never figured greatly in my life. Now papayas were everywhere I was.

My preoccupation with papayas didn't hit me all at once. A few nagging questions only gradually turned into a full-scale fixation. It's not that I was especially interested in consuming papayas, which I think taste like a vague memory of something that tastes a lot stronger; it's that I grew increasingly determined to understand the phenomenology of papayas in New York. How did a tropical fruit come to be so prominent in a temperate-zone city? Why were there so *many* papaya stores? Why did all of them sell frankfurters too? (I mean, were they health-food stores or junk-food stores?) Why did so many papaya stores include references to royalty in their names? Why were all of them decorated with signs using stilted, hyperbolic descriptions of papayas, like THE ARISTOCTATIC MELON OF THE TROPICS, THE FAMOUS MAGICAL PAPAYA MELON, and GOD'S GIFT TO MANKIND IS OUR PAPAYA DRINK? That nobody I knew could answer these questions, or had even considered them, came as no particular surprise; one characteristic of the New York personality I had noticed right away was an ability to overlook prevailing conditions, such as high taxes and sidewalk bridges. Papayas seemed to be just another prevailing condition.

I did what I could to get answers. I put questions to countermen at various papaya outposts and got strangely specific but unsubstantiated reactions, among them "Eighty-five percent of all people in the world love papaya" (the bun man at Papaya Kingdom) and "The relationship between the hot dog and the papaya is very good" (the juice man at Gray's). I also talked to Peter Poulos, the owner of Papaya King, which, I learned, was the original papaya store in New York. He said that his father had traveled to Florida decades earlier and had come back fired up with the idea of introducing New Yorkers to the tropical delights of papaya juice. The outbreak of other papaya stores, he said, was an attempt to copy Papaya King's success. The romantic paeans to the papaya were his father's own words and cadence, and the other stores just duplicated them. The other stores' references to royalty were meant to fool customers into thinking that all the papaya stores were affiliated, like some tropical-fruit-juice House of Hapsburg.

A few days after talking to Mr. Poulos, I came across a United States District Court opinion in a 1989 case involving Papaya King and

Papaya Kingdom. The former had charged the latter with trademark infringement, on the ground that the papaya-plus-royalty name implied that the two businesses were associated. Papaya King had won. The owners of Papaya Kingdom then tried to satisfy the judgment by merely covering up the *K* on its sign with a piece of tape. Peter Leisure, the judge in the case, observed wryly that the defendant was "contented apparently to be known as 'Papaya ingdom.'" Less wryly, he imposed contempt charges on Papaya Kingdom—or, rather, Papaya ingdom: twenty-five thousand dollars in damages, seventy-five hundred for contempt of court, and more than thirteen thousand in attorneys' fees. I went down to Papaya ingdom a few days after reading the opinion to see whether the store had a new name and a new sign. It was gone, and a pizzeria had risen in its place.

It was at about this time that I began to get used to living here: I knew uptown from downtown, and I had finally figured out that the guys in my parking garage were denting my car because I hadn't tipped them, and I had come to realize that there were certain things about the city that I would never understand. I wouldn't say I gave up; I simply started taking things in stride. This was when Gray's was selling its frankfurters for fifty cents (they're now $1.95), and business was particularly brisk; I rarely passed by when a House o' Weenies truck wasn't double-parked by the door, offloading product. (I never saw anything like a House o' Tropical Fruits truck parked nearby, so I assumed that the papayas were delivered late at night—just the way you'd expect exotic cargo to arrive.) I still dropped in for a hot dog now and then, but I stopped pestering the countermen with questions about papayas. The crowd at Gray's was always the same peculiar mixture of panhandlers, with barely enough money for a Gray's special (two frankfurters and a papaya drink for two dollars), working people in a hurry, and one or two anxious-looking guys in suits. No one ever talked to anyone, and the radio was always blasting country music. I no longer drove myself crazy trying to figure out this combination of the tropics, street life, hot dogs, and Loretta Lynn. It had become a part of my neighborhood, period. In some ways, I felt relieved.

One day at Gray's, I ordered a hot dog and a small papaya—I had finally come around to drinking papaya juice—and got in line for the mustard, which was in a stout gallon jug with a plastic squirt top. The man behind me was skinny and bedraggled, and in my best I'm-a-New-Yorker-now style, I pretended he didn't exist. I certainly expected that, in keeping with the custom at Gray's, we wouldn't converse. As we waited for the mustard though, he leaned over my shoulder and muttered to me, "It's going to blow up." I took a deep breath and looked away. "It's going to blow up," he repeated. I tried to look more explicitly uninterested. Garrulous strangers with the urge to share their apocalyptic visions appeared often enough in my day-to-day life so that I had gotten good at this; in fact, I took pride in staying unruffled. I was now just one person away from the mustard, and I planned to dress my dog quickly and find a place at the window far from the skinny man. He said it again, this time very distinctly: "Hey. It's. Going. To. Blow. *Up.*"

It was my turn. I set my papaya juice down on the counter, positioned my hot dog under the nozzle, and pressed down hard on the top. It blew up. Mustard splattered all over my hands and my shirt. Most of the hot dog remained naked; the bun had a small mustard-filled crater, made by the impact. A plug of dried mustard that had caused the explosion was somewhere east of my papaya juice. "I *told* you it was going to blow up," the man said, shaking his head.

I looked at him and said apologetically, "I just moved here."

ME LOVE BROOKLYN

Adam Sternbergh

My first apartment in New York City was in Brooklyn, near Atlantic Terminal, so my commute to work took me on the D train across the Manhattan Bridge. As you cross over the bridge on the subway, the view in either direction is dazzling; it feels like you're riding between two giant propped-up postcards. To the north: the iron latticework of the Williamsburg Bridge, the smokestacks of industrial Brooklyn, and the westward curve of the East River. To the south: the world-famous Brooklyn Bridge, the world-famouser Statue of Liberty; and the sun-snatching towers rising up in downtown Manhattan. In between it all: you, on your first subway ride to a brand-new job in New York City.

Naturally, the first time I saw this, I was awestruck, but no one else on the train could give a shit. Of course not: only tourists jump up to catch the view on a Monday morning subway ride, and unlike me, the rest of these riders were already New Yorkers. They were lost in the thrum of the morning commute, buried in newspapers or novels or naps. (This was 2004, years before iPhones and Angry Birds became the commuters' distraction of choice.) But on the first morning that I took that ride, still living among unpacked cardboard boxes just recently shipped south from Toronto, I told myself that if I ever found that this view no longer thrilled me, I'd know it was time for me to leave New York.

Everyone who moves to New York from another place comes at least in part because they're chasing after an idea of "New York." This New York is not a place you move to; you actually arrive with it already in your mind. This New York has only a tangential relationship to the actual bricks-and-mortar city; instead, it's constructed from a collection of movie scenes, Broadway song lyrics, half-remembered punk albums, and/or favorite dog-eared novels devoured over the years. Your personal New York might roughly resemble the one in *The Sweet Smell of Success* or the one in *Wall Street* or the one in *Sex and the City*—all very different cities—but it's also just that: yours. You built it. It's a kind of mental collage you've assembled over the years, then decided you should find a way to live inside.

Before I moved here, when I was living in Toronto, I'd long been obsessed with New York as a quasi-mythical magic city that somehow also existed in real life. Sure, New York is where Woody Allen lives, but just as important, it's where Spider-Man lives as well. My personal New York, the one I was chasing, was not surprisingly one we can roughly classify as Literary New York—you know, the city where Hart Crane throws a drink in Norman Mailer's face at an overcrowded Upper West Side cocktail party, while George Plimpton bores Mary McCarthy by reciting that same anecdote yet again, and Toni Morrison debates the honesty of metaphors with Paul Auster on the fire escape after he slips out to smoke a cigarillo. (I don't even know what the honesty of metaphors means; I can barely hear their conversation over the din of the party.) This is the New York of snappy dialogue and clattering typewriters and late nights at Elaine's restaurant and Dorothy Parker zingers. In real New York, though, I soon found out, there are few typewriters, clattering or otherwise; Dorothy Parker is dead and Elaine's is now closed; and the dialogue you hear is often distressingly flat and predictable, especially coming from your own mouth.

And if you're not careful, you can spend, and waste, a lot of your time in this actual city, especially when you first arrive, scrambling after your idea of New York—the one that lured you here and which can seem, once you arrive, as elusive as a great party you were thrilled to be invited to, yet for which you now realize you've lost the address, though you're absolutely sure has got to be *somewhere* on this block. (Maybe it's behind that lit-up second-story window? Or if I just follow that clamorous din? Or that gang of cool-looking people— where are they headed?) As a result, you might fritter away a lot of time in really loud Lower East Side bars or really expensive West Village bistros or really stuffy Upper East Side cocktail parties or really far-flung precincts of Brooklyn (Williamsburg . . . no, Bushwick . . . no, Ridgewood?), always confident that the New York you're pining for is just around the next corner. I mean, it's got to be around here somewhere, right? Because if it's not in New York, then where could it be?

Moving to actual New York is not romantic, it's hard, especially if you do it alone. Not long after I arrived, I bought a mug from a local coffee shop called Gorilla Coffee; the mug featured a picture of the Brooklyn Bridge, a gorilla, and a thought bubble coming out of the gorilla that read, ME LOVE BROOKLYN. I think I bought that mug mostly to convince myself that, like the gorilla, I did too. Ten years and innumerable dishwashings later, the message on that mug—ME LOVE BROOKLYN—has only half faded away.

Otherwise, in that time, I've formed, or continue to form, a very different opinion of living in New York, the actual city. To paraphrase Winston Churchill's famous observation about democracy: New York City is the worst place in the world to live, except for all the others.

Why is this? Well, I often tell people who ask about living in New York (usually breathless visitors who've hijacked my couch for a week) that the very things that make it such an exciting city to visit—the crowds, the ceaseless onslaught of enticing events, the overall energizing electricity of the city—can make it a huge pain in the ass to actually live in. New York is a city where there are always a million exciting things to do at any given moment, and a million other people who are doing them at the exact same moment as you are. That hot new play? Already sold out. That enticing MoMA exhibit? At last report, the wait is over twelve hours. How about something simple, like a blanket, a bottle of wine, and a nightfall screening of *Paper Moon* in Bryant Park? Sure, if you don't mind homesteading a coffin-sized plot of grass at around four in the afternoon, then fending off claim jumpers for the next five hours until sundown. That's assuming, of course, you have any time left over to do any of this when you're not either working or drinking to work off the edge from the working or trying to do regular-life kinds of stuff like buying groceries and picking up dry cleaning.

And if that whole spiel hasn't scared the person off (or at least off my couch), I'll then follow up with this:

I often think that, in many ways, moving to New York is like dating the best-looking, most popular girl (or boy) in your high school. In some respect it's something you logically and understandably might want to do. And once you do it, you will definitely feel proud that you have achieved this accomplishment, and others, who are not dating that girl (or boy), may well look upon you with envy. But there is a trade-off, and the trade-off is this: You will get to see—nay, will be forced to see, every single day—just exactly what that girl (or boy) is made of. All the blemishes that aren't visible when gazed upon from a distance. All the annoying tics and flaws that can only really grate on you once you experience them intimately and repeatedly. My point being, what seemed so alluring in theory can often be tiresome and troubling in practice.

. . .

For a long time after I first moved to New York, I was bolstered by those rare and invaluable moments when the city does deign to show you a glimpse of its fabled magic, like a dour maiden clad in heavy velvet who shows a glimpse of heel. I collected these moments and clung to them as a ballast against despair, even as I waited for that one boffo moment, the real showstopper, that would justify all the daily grinding down. You know the kind of moment I mean: I wanted to see Woody Allen wrestling the Angel of Bethesda over the fountain in Central Park. I wanted to walk the Brooklyn Bridge with Walt Whitman while he composed a poem about it in real time. I wanted to grow up to be the fourth Beastie Boy. I wanted to live next door to CBGB's back when it was a punk bar and not a punk-bar-themed clothing store.

But it turns out I never had a moment like this. My New York moments were quieter. Moments like these: Leaving work one night in Midtown late during one of those weird intemperate maritime weather spells when fog sneaks around the city, and seeing—stumbling on, really, insofar as you can stumble on a skyscraper—Rockefeller Center, rising out of the mist like a spotlit, art deco–era movie star on opening night.

Or seeing the Chrysler Building anytime, in any weather.

Or the time on the D train when we pulled into Broadway-Lafayette station, and the doors opened, and there was a busker on the platform singing what I guessed was an old Italian folk song, and an elderly man sitting next to me, silent during the ride until now, recognized the song and joined in, singing along in full voice.

Or watching Meryl Streep in *Mother Courage* outdoors on a perfect summer night in Central Park, and missing pretty much the entire play because you're busy thinking, "Holy shit, I'm watching Meryl Streep in *Mother Courage* outdoors on a perfect summer night in

Central Park." And falling in love with New York, and summertime, and Central Park, and Meryl Streep, in roughly that order.

Or walking through a snowstorm on the closing night of my then-girlfriend, now-wife's play, performed upstairs at Saint Mark's Church, where the house was full despite the blizzard, because people do that kind of thing in New York, and it also happened to be my birthday, so afterward we walked to a local bar, and the streets were empty and snow-buried, with fat flakes falling everywhere, and the city was the quietest I'd ever heard it, and nearly the prettiest too.

Or the time I saw, one morning on the subway riding into Manhattan from Brooklyn, an Orthodox Jewish man hunched over his weathered prayer book, chanting at a murmur, davening and rocking back and forth. And sitting right next to him was a young black kid, wearing headphones as big as kaiser rolls, listening to something with an obviously infectious beat. And both their heads were bobbing until, for one magical synchronous moment, like an Art Spiegelman *New Yorker* cover come to life, their heads started to bob in time. The two of them, alone and together, falling into the rhythm of the city, and then it was gone as quickly as it came.

And what I finally realized is that the small encounters you have with the city gradually come to crowd out the romantic ideas you clung to; that as in any long and fulfilling and treasured relationship, what you come to value most are not the illusions you arrived with but the experiences you've accumulated.

So here's my real New York moment: it was the first time I took that D train ride over the Manhattan Bridge and didn't look up. Because that was the moment I stopped chasing New York and started living here.

NEW YORK COOL

Sari Botton

1.

When I was thirteen and a half, I was allowed for the first time to go to Manhattan unchaperoned by an adult, and it changed me.

I went with my cousin, who was fourteen. The plan was to get together with friends from summer camp, some of whom were boys a couple of years older. We assured our parents we were in good hands; those guys knew how to navigate the buses and subways, and presumably everything else in life. I had no idea what we were going to *do* there and was fairly anxious about that, as I was about most things. But for the first time I felt like a teenager and not a little kid, grownup and sophisticated, even though before we boarded the LIRR, my mother safety-pinned a five-dollar bill into each of our front pockets in case we were mugged.

We didn't do anything special with our friends that day, mostly just walked around the Village. There were six or seven of us casually bouncing from record store to pizza parlor to head shop to a boutique on MacDougal Street called Reminiscence, where the girls among us would spend our babysitting money on the store's famously inexpensive brightly colored carpenter pants. We hung out in Washington Square Park near the fountain, huddling around the guitar players strumming folk songs and singing along. We thought that was the coolest. We were too young and uninitiated then to know how uncool and touristy a New York City cliché that was.

It was the first time I'd ever gone to the city to do *nothing in particular*, and that detail alone initiated a shifting in my sense of myself. With my family, I'd gone to plays, Lincoln Center, museums, the circus. This was different. We were just bumming around, but it was the most exciting thing in the world to me because we were on our own, and because without a particular destination, you didn't know where you were going to land or what you were going to see. I tried to seem blasé about it, though. There was something inherently blasé about coming to the city to do nothing in particular, wasn't there? No big deal. I'm just walking around the city with my friends. I'm cool. I'd never felt the slightest bit cool before. I'd felt decidedly *uncool* and anxious about it.

As we traipsed around the park, an assortment of men passed us by, shifting their eyes, not turning their heads, asking each of us under their breath, "Want a lude?" I kept hearing it, over and over. *Want a lude? Want a lude? Want a lude?* By the fountain, by the playground, by the chess tables, by the arch. *Want a lude? Want a lude?*

I tried not to react. I didn't want to let on to my friends that I was so inexperienced as to have not even the vaguest idea what that was. I knew enough from the suspicious way the men asked that it was probably something drug related and assumed my friends knew what it was. Most of them were smoking pot already, or had at least tried it. I had not.

Or could it have been sex related? Were those men offering a *lewd*?

I waited until my cousin and I were on the train home to ask her plainly, "What's a lude?"

She cocked her head, scrunched up her nose, and thought for a second.

"I'm pretty sure it's a thing you use to put the pot in the joint," she said.

I wasn't convinced. I didn't say anything, though, just nodded.

When we got home, I asked, "Dad, what's a lude?" Needless to say, we were forbidden from visiting the city unchaperoned again for a long time.

2.

That's when I started sneaking in on my own, walking around and doing nothing in particular, just absorbing the city's cityness, letting it keep changing me. I often say that New York City is where I became *me*. (I hear others say this, too.) It was in those days that it began.

I wanted desperately to be changed, to feel and be different. I was so unsure of myself—an awkward mix of extrovert and introvert, loner and social butterfly. As a daughter of clergy and teachers, I was rewarded again and again for being "good" and "nice" and asking for little, and I became so detached from my needs, instincts, and desires that it would take me decades (and countless shrink sessions) to recognize them. I felt out of step with my peers, who were less afraid to experiment with independence and rebellion—who were familiar with current music, while I grew up in a house filled with opera, show tunes, and pop standards. If the music you listened to determined how cool you were, I was doomed. An older friend—a surrogate brother, really—began making me mix tapes to bring me up to speed. "Just be yourself," he'd advise me again and again when I confided about not knowing how to behave socially. *Be myself?* I had no idea who that was.

In order to figure it out, I needed to observe others, and in a place where I wasn't being watched closely, so I could worry less about being "good." (Not that I really did anything "bad." I didn't drink or do drugs, and to this day I have never smoked a single cigarette.) Where better to do that than the capital of cool? I'd ride the train in and walk around studying people, searching for clues about *how to be*—how to be anyone but dorky, insecure me. How to be the kind of cool, jaded New Yorker who knew what a "lude" was, and whether or not she wanted one.

3.

Two years later, when I was fifteen, I began traveling into the city *chaperoned*, one evening a week to attend Hebrew school—"confirmation class."

I was instantly uncomfortable in my surroundings, a room full of prep school kids. I was one of the few who didn't show up dressed in a school uniform—crisply ironed oxford shirts, wool skirts, trousers, monogrammed blazers. I was sure it signified that I was the only one who wasn't rich, something I was painfully self-conscious about. I'd grown up adjacent to the affluence and privilege of camp friends, kids from neighboring towns, relatives and step-relatives, while my immediate family never really had money, both my parents needing to work multiple jobs.

With the other kids all attending fancy schools with stuffy-sounding names like Dalton, Birch Wathen, Horace Mann, Fieldston, and Brearley, I expected religious school in Manhattan to be dork city. But I was wrong. Those kids were the coolest. They could go out to nightclubs and bars without needing anything but obviously very fake IDs. (Bear in mind, this was 1980, and the drinking age in New York was eighteen.) They could go to someplace called Film Forum, which came up a lot among a certain subset when they gabbed before and after class and during break. They could go out *anywhere* in the city, and without having to ask their parents to drive them. They knew how to take the subway alone and weren't afraid of it. They listened to Lou Reed, Patti Smith, and John Coltrane. The girls smoked clove cigarettes. And they all knew that "lude" was short for Quaalude, the tranquilizer of choice among recreational users at clubs like Studio 54, which some of my classmates had been to. (A year later I'd try unsuccessfully to get in there with a couple of other kids from Long Island.)

I observed them closely, listened to their conversations, envied their independence and sophistication. There was no way I was going to get in with them. I didn't even bother to try. Which is why I was surprised when one of the boys tried to convince me to join them on the youth group retreat in the Berkshires—I didn't go—and then one of the girls invited me to a sleepover party at her family's gaping Upper East Side apartment when her parents were away in Europe.

"Okay," I said. "Do I need to bring, like, a sleeping bag?"

"No," she told me. "We have a lot of beds and stuff."

The party turned out to be a big bash, the sleepover part inadvertently coed. I tried to act as if that was normal in suburbia too. There were some kids there from Hebrew school but also a lot of others whom I'd never met before. I didn't quite know where to put myself. Everyone at the party was out of my league, in every possible way— they were moneyed, they knew how to mix drinks (none of which I wanted anyway), they were having sex, they were culturally aware. I stumbled upon a conversation in the kitchen about someone called Godard. I had no idea who Godard was—and because they kept dropping perfectly inflected French into the conversation, and not the *Voilà Madame et Monsieur Thibaud* kind of French I was learning on Long Island, I had no idea whether Godard was a he or a she or a musician or a poet, or their French teacher, so I left the room. I was too shy to speak most of the night, and then afterward, through the rest of the Hebrew school year.

Our teacher noticed and pulled me aside one day. "Don't let those kids intimidate you just because they're especially erudite."

"Okay," I said.

He thought for a moment.

"Do you know what erudite means?"

"Of course," I lied.

I didn't necessarily like those kids. I didn't know them well enough to say for sure. But their cultural awareness, their worldliness, their self-assuredness, their *eruditeness*—their cool New Yorkerness— made an impression on me. I wanted to be like them. I wanted to live in the city someday. I just had to.

4.

And so I did, in a variety of neighborhoods—the East Village, then Yorkville, then the Upper West Side, and finally back to the East Village, where I stayed for roughly a dozen years.

More than just New York City in general, the East Village is where I became *me*, although it took me some time. I got a railroad apartment there in the early nineties, and like so many who move there, I saw it as an opportunity to reinvent myself. Goodbye, parent-fearing goody- two-shoes self-conscious loner theater geek from Long Island. I was on my way to becoming . . . well, I still didn't know what or who exactly, but some kind of cool New Yorker.

I looked to the East Village as my very own dork rehabilitation program, designed to obliterate the scars of having grown up one of the teachers' kids in a rough blue-collar town on Long Island—home of Henry Hill of *Goodfellas* fame—filled with tough kids, some of them from families on the lowest rungs of the Mafia totem pole.

I'd often overhear the popular kids at school self-consciously gauging their coolness relative to one another. "You go to the city? Yeah? Where you go?" CBGB's, Max's Kansas City, the Mudd Club, even the folky bars on Bleecker Street were answers that would put you in pretty good standing. As opposed to: confirmation class. Or a "sing-in" at Merkin Concert Hall, where operatic vocalists fill the seats and sing along to Handel's *Messiah*, with your dad in the baritone section. Bonus dork points if you're at the sing-in instead of hanging out uptown with your friends, who are having the once-in-a-lifetime experience of attending the vigil for John Lennon in Central Park.

But now I *lived* in the city. So there. Not that it made me feel any more sure of myself. Not right away, anyway.

Once again, I found myself studying people for clues as to *how to be*, this time the outspoken, often pierced and tattooed and Manic Panic–dyed women writers, artists, poets, and singers I came across at places like the Nuyorican Poets Café, Sidewalk, a grungy coffeehouse on Avenue A called Limbo, and Deanna's, a jazz club on East Seventh Street where there were poetry readings on Sundays. That's the first place I heard the famous slam poet Maggie Estep, who died, tragically, in 2014 from a sudden heart attack.

5.

That was not the first time I'd caught sight of Maggie Estep. I can't recall the specific moment when I first encountered her somewhere in the East Village. I'm not sure whether it was before or after I'd caught her hilarious spoken-word MTV video for "Hey, Baby," off her *No More Mister Nice Girl* record. The one where she takes a lewd, crotch-grabbing catcaller completely off guard with a brilliantly absurd response—basically, saying, "Sure, that sounds good, let's go back to my place . . ."

For some reason I have it in my mind that I *hadn't* yet known, the first time I spotted Maggie, that she was famous, that you didn't need to know that in order to get what a cool New Yorker she was, to be impressed by the confident way she stomped around the city in a fitted black dress, fishnets, and combat boots, her full lips coated in that matte cinnabar red that was popular then, her expression equal parts "Look at me" and "Who the fuck are *you* looking at?"

I was in my midtwenties then, just a couple of years younger than Maggie. I'm embarrassed to admit that before seeing the video for "Hey, Baby" on MTV, it hadn't occurred to me to feel anything but flattered and validated when men on the street catcalled. Before hearing her perform her poem "The Stupid Jerk I'm Obsessed With," it hadn't quite dawned on me that I had one (or more) of those too.

I didn't know Maggie yet, but I looked up to her. Knowing that she lived in the East Village like I did made me feel like a cool New Yorker by association. She seemed genuinely to not give a shit what you thought of her, and that, more than anything, made her cool—not just *tough* cool, not aloof for the sake of being cool, but *self-possessed* cool. *New York* cool.

I found it impossible to master that. For the longest time, I still gave a shit, a *sizeable* shit, about what people thought of me, kept aggressively trying to up my coolness quotient. For a while, I felt as if it was working. When I went to see one of the stupid jerks I was obsessed with play with his band at downtown nightclubs, I met editors from *Billboard* and *Rolling Stone* and started writing about music and nightlife for them, the *New York Times*, and soon MTV News. But first and foremost, I was a musical theater geek, a lover of standards and show tunes. I was now familiar with a lot more music than I'd been as a kid, and I could enjoy and appreciate much of it. But I felt like a complete fraud acting as any kind of authority or arbiter in the rock and rap worlds. I had to do a Nexis search every time I was assigned another musician or band to write about, just to find out who they were. This was me trying to be cool, which was, of course, the opposite of cool. I had to quit that work. It wasn't me. I'd go into ghostwriting instead—

which, well, obviously that really wasn't being me either, but in a different way—and copywriting.

6.

In the summer of 2003, I had a freelance copywriting gig at an ad agency on Twenty-Sixth and Broadway. On nice days, I'd bring my lunch to Madison Square Park and people-watch as I ate. I was, by that point, an adept people watcher. Having been at it since I was a teen, I knew how to study people without making them feel as if they were under the microscope.

I'd also developed radar for New York people with whom you'd want to avoid eye contact, and therefore not observe too closely. There were the obvious ones—the crazies yelling at no one in particular; people with clipboards, who invariably try to get you to do something, like sign a petition, go to a comedy club, or try a new hair salon. And then there were the more subtle cases—guys who were always on the lookout for women to hit on; the kinds of lonely New Yorkers who will talk (and talk and talk) to anyone who'll listen.

At first glance, I regarded the group of pimply born-again evangelist teens on a mission from the Bible Belt as best to avoid. They'd been making their way around the park at lunchtime for several days, spreading the Good News dressed in matching brightly colored T-shirts emblazoned with the name of their South Carolina church. My aversion wasn't merely due to having been raised Jewish; I also made it my business to steer clear of the roving Lubavitcher Mitzvah Tank every time I caught sight of it, and the black-clad men around it asking passersby, "Are you Jewish?" I'm put off by proselytization and allergic, non-denominationally, to religion in general.

But one particularly beautiful day when I didn't feel like going back to a dimly lit, stuffy office just yet, I didn't look away when I saw three of the girls approaching my vicinity. One of them locked eyes with me, and instead of getting up and leaving, I waited for them.

"Hi, can we talk to you?" one of them drawled. My inner awkward teen admired how bold and forthcoming she was. It must have been nice to have a legitimate reason to approach people. I thought about my own eye-opening experiences as a teen in New York. How might their experiences here change them?

"Sure," I said. "You can talk to me."

"Are you Christian?"

"No."

"Are you Catholic?"

"No."

"Are you Jewish?"

"No."

They were running out of options, and I wasn't being completely straight with them.

"Well," I allowed, "I was raised Jewish, but I don't practice. I'm *culturally* Jewish, though. Like, *New York* Jewish."

The girls looked puzzled. "Well, what do you *believe in*?"

I took a deep breath and tried to recall how I'd filled in the religion portion of my online dating profile, still active at the time. "Um, I believe in . . . the interconnectedness of everything . . . ?"

They were silent for a moment. "What does *that* mean?"

Did I even know what that meant? "It means I think we're all—everyone in the world—part of something larger, together. And that everything each one of us does affects everyone and everything *else*, so we have to consider how we live in the world in those terms. That's my religion." They looked perplexed.

"Well, do you believe in heaven?"

"No, not really. I think we have to live for now."

"Do you believe in *hell*? And the *devil*?" They were getting exasperated.

"Well, actually, I don't believe in 'good' and 'bad.'"

This was just too much. Their eyes got big. When they'd approached me, they'd had no idea that they were signing up for a Talmudic debate with a heathen. I started to feel sorry for them but was in too deep to drop my argument.

"See, I prefer not to ascribe values like that to things." This wasn't helping. I tried harder. "What's *bad* for one person is *good* for another. There's nothing that's inherently, universally *good*, and nothing that's inherently, universally *bad*, as far as I'm concerned."

Now I'd crossed a line.

"Oh, yeah? Well, what about 9/11?" one of the girls shrieked. "And Osama Bin Laden?" yelled another.

I'd really struck a nerve. I wondered how much further to take this. "Okay, yeah, 9/11 was horrific, no doubt about that," I started. "But we've done a lot of bad things to people in other countries. Sometimes we do *bad* things to people in other countries so that we can have things back home that we think are *good*."

"So you're admitting there *are* such things as good and bad?" one of them quickly challenged me. She was all worked up now.

"Well, not entirely," I said. "Sometimes so-called good things come about because of so-called bad ones, and vice versa. So who's to say which is which?"

Tired of arguing, I found myself telling them about the aftermath of 9/11, when people in my world came together in way I'd never experienced before. I had been feeling as if the city wasn't really home anymore and thinking about leaving. My life there had become routine. I'd been emotionally gutted by a breakup six months prior. I worked all the time and never seemed to get ahead. I felt disconnected from friends, painfully alone. The city was all hard edges.

"But after 9/11, people let their guards down and really reached out. People took care of one another." I told them about the impromptu, mournful potluck dinners where we grieved together because it was all too much to handle alone; the check-in phone calls between neighbors who'd never spoken before and between old friends who'd lost contact; the kind gestures among strangers.

The girls stood there, utterly stumped. Finally one of them spoke. "Is it all right if we pray for you?"

On my walk back to the office, I realized I needed to expand my criteria for what it meant to be a cool New Yorker. People often mistake New Yorkers for rude and mean, but they're really just no-nonsense and efficient. They don't have time, regularly, to be warm and friendly with everyone who crosses their path. Nothing would ever get done. But when the chips are down, when it matters, they drop their cool exteriors and become unabashedly human.

I also realized I had just delivered the kind of philosophical mind-fuck that only a true cool, jaded New Yorker can. No doubt about it; I was the real deal now.

7.

I don't remember how or when, but at some point in my thirties I stopped caring about whether I was cool, or a real New Yorker, rather than Long Island "bridge and tunnel." That's probably when I dropped all the pretension and *became* a real New Yorker by way of just being *me*. At that advanced age, so much later than it happens for others, it finally dawned on me that, duh, being cool had nothing to do with being a music journalist or knowing about French film or combat boots or piercings or tattoos—although I would get a tattoo years later, on my right forearm, on the eve of my forty-seventh birthday. A corny, uncool one at that—an Anaïs Nin quote that you likely come across all the time on mugs and magnets and the covers of journals and all other manner of inspirational doodads: "And the day came when the risk to remain tight in a bud was more painful than the risk it took to blossom." I didn't care that it was corny and uncool. That wasn't why I was getting it. I was getting it to embolden myself to *be myself*, unapologetically, unabashedly, even when that meant seeming uncool, or in any way different from how others wanted me to be. (I teach a writing workshop at an upstate jail for teen boys, most of them from the city. Typically, when they first spot my tattoo, they're impressed and ask to see it. But after they've looked at it up close and I've explained it to them, they express their disappointment: "*Aw*, Miss. I thought you were cool.")

I'll admit, though, that leaving New York City, as I did nine years ago after losing my apartment and moving upstate, elicited a certain anxiety about my ability to retain whatever coolness factor fifteen years there had bestowed upon me. I like to believe that once a New Yorker, always a New Yorker. That the city changes you, irreversibly.

There are moments, though, when I realize I'm completely out of the loop with things happening in the city. So many of my favorite places are gone. I don't know where to eat or hang out—I have to figure it out each time I take the bus down. There's still a thrill in not knowing where I'll land, but it's tempered by an old, familiar insecurity. In those moments I worry, Am I clueless? Am I a hick now? Have I lost all my cred?

But a couple of years ago, when the nonprofit storytelling organization I'm involved with held a story slam at a nightclub in Kingston, I was given a glimmer of hope that has mostly stuck with me. I was taken aback by one of the names on the sign-up list: Maggie Estep.

Could it be *that* Maggie Estep? I wondered. The person who first popularized and pretty much came to personify slams in general? The performer who covered Lou Reed's "Vicious" in a music video directed by Steve Buscemi, in which Lou Reed himself appears? (*Because he asked if he could.*) The cool New Yorker I'd idolized?

Sure enough, it was *that* Maggie Estep. Although, more demure in look and tone than I'd remembered, her shiny black hair cropped short into a modern gamine cut. She read from *Diary of an Emotional Idiot*, one of the seven critically acclaimed novels she'd written since her slam poetry days.

I learned that evening that Maggie had left the city and moved upstate two years after I did and never looked back. Knowing that, I thought, Okay. Maybe I am still a little cool.

THE SHVITZ AT THE END OF THE WORLD

Brian Macaluso

It was 1999, the end of the millennium. Added to all the excitement was the terror of something ominous called "Y2K" approaching. An oversight in the keeping of computer time threatened to make entire networks across the globe go haywire at the stroke of midnight on New Year's Eve. We were warned it might cause bank vaults to open, prison security systems to fail, airplanes to drop from the sky, nuclear missiles to launch. It was an apocalyptic time, if you were inclined to believe the hype.

The national news wasn't just dystopian but sordid too. The Monica Lewinsky scandal was still a relevant topic, President Clinton having only recently narrowly escaped impeachment.

I was living in New York City, newly single and having a hard time of things. I'd never felt more alone. I'd been dumped by my fiancée, all my friends had moved, the recording industry—the field I worked in and loved—was in free fall, and in response, I was struggling to establish my own IT consulting business.

Y2K loomed particularly large in light of my relatively new profession. I spent many months racing to prevent whatever cataclysms it threatened to bring to my customers. I felt as if all I did was work and was extremely stressed out. When you live in New York City and do nothing but work, eat, and sleep when you can, it becomes a very dark, depressing place. Whatever charms it's held for you seem to disappear from memory. It takes a deep toll, and one day I just hit a wall. I simply couldn't work, and so I gave up and treated myself to a rare indulgence: I took the day off and went to the shvitz.

"The shvitz" is how regulars refer to what is more formally known as the Russian Turkish Baths, or the Tenth Street Baths. A local institution situated in a slightly decrepit tenement building on East Tenth Street near Avenue A in the East Village, it is rife with history and gossip, dating back to 1862. The place was rumored, at one time, to be owned by the Russian mob. Speculation had the place as a front for drug running, money laundering, prostitution, and other shady dealings. I never believed it. I would just occasionally unassumingly pay my twenty-five bucks for the day and sweat and let myself be transported by the old-world feel.

I entered the main floor, flashed my membership card, and put my valuables in the antique safe-deposit box behind the check-in counter. I can't remember whether it was a Boris card or a David card I had; there was and probably remains an epic feud between Boris and David, the two owners. They alternated weeks as operators of the place, and if you wanted to go on a Boris week, you had to have a Boris card, and vice versa. It somehow added to the place's peculiar appeal.

You also had to keep track of whether it was a coed day or one of the days that were exclusively for men or for women, to accommodate the religious Jews who frequented the shvitz.

I took my locker key, grabbed a ratty towel, a threadbare robe and shorts, and cheap-ass flip-flops, got changed, and headed to the basement. The basement is where it all happens.

This being the basement of an East Village tenement building, it's not that big. Crammed into it is the sauna, the Turkish steam room, the regular steam room, the cold pool, where you can freeze your nads off, and my favorite, the Russian radiant sauna.

"The Russian room," as it's more commonly called, is basically a concrete bunker with three tiers of benches all facing a huge furnace, which has been burning all the previous night. Spigots of cold water every five feet fill buckets for patrons to cool off with in the 130-degree heat. A little piece of Hell. It's fucking great.

It was the middle of the week, so the place wasn't too crowded. Sitting in the Russian room, I felt myself begin to relax. But if I was going to really refresh and rejuvenate, to use holistic spa parlance, I knew I'd need to do more. I had to make it my business to really decompress and clear my mind so that in the following days, I could save the world—well, my little world—from the Y2K monster. I mean, I owed it to my customers, didn't I? I decided that indeed I did, and so I booked myself two treatments: a platza and a black mud treatment. Why not? I had all day.

The platza treatment is essentially getting beaten and whipped for twenty minutes with two pom-poms made of oak leaves dunked in scalding-hot soapy water. It's very satisfying, in a masochistic sort of way, the kind of spa experience only a true stressed-out New Yorker can appreciate. Said to open the pores and allow toxins to be released, it's performed on the topmost bench in the lung-searingly hot Russian room, for all to see, by a middle-aged deaf guy who likely has been born into the trade. The experience is very old-world. Also great.

The black mud treatment takes place in a bleak, industrial-looking private space with all the charm of a restaurant dishwashing room. It involves hot, foul-smelling mud allegedly from the Dead Sea applied to your naked body by a very large and robust Russian woman, and then allowed to cure into sarcophagus hardness before being washed off by a fire hose.

During the application process, this woman sort of reached down and . . . tweaked me . . . down there. I figured it had happened inadvertently as she was putting on the mud and tried to turn my mind from it. (I did, however, have a most normal warm-blooded healthy male reaction to being tweaked.) To my relief, the treatment went on without incident. All in all, it was quite relaxing. I even fell asleep for a while before getting hosed down.

Afterward, I went back into the Russian room and shvitzed some more. Then I jumped in the cold pool and went back and forth a few more times. It all felt so great. I didn't want to leave this underground paradise. And so I decided to really get the most from the day and booked a massage.

Why the hell not? I thought. It's my day off and Y2K is coming. The world might be ending. Who knows whether I'll ever get to do this again?

I was instructed to go upstairs to the treatment area and was given a room number. I entered the room, got undressed, and waited on the table for my massage therapist.

Who should come in but the tweaker! She proceeded to give me the kind of massage that only a large, robust Russian woman can give. She wielded her arms like rolling pins and I turned to pretzel dough. I dozed off and woke when I sensed she was just about done. It was a pretty great massage. It left me deeply relaxed. Now I'd surely be in better shape for battling the largest computer glitch to ever threaten New York City, let alone the globe.

I started to get up, but the masseuse leaned over and whispered in my ear.

"Would you like a Clinton massage?"

A *what*?

"A Clinton massage."

Oh . . . a *Clinton* massage . . .

I won't say what happened. But I will say that this story has a happy ending.

QUIT EVERYTHING

Kathleen Hale

I used to live near the Gowanus Canal, in a redbrick stump of a building that was squashed between a Laundromat and a chicken slaughterhouse. Dry-cleaning exhaust hung above the stop sign at the corner and collected in a white film on the sidewalk. Most evenings, I deliberately passed the apartment on my way home from work, trudging all the way to the corner just to fill my lungs with soapy fumes, which offered welcome relief from the reek of burnt feathers downwind.

Every morning at 7:30 a.m., I skidded downhill through slippery dregs of chicken innards and bolted for the R train, which always lurched into view late and farting sparks. I hated my job—plus my live-in boyfriend, Jonathan, rarely wanted to kiss me anymore. The unpredictable schedule of the R train only added to my overall confusion and mounting panic. No matter how I planned my mornings, I always seemed to arrive at the turnstile just in time to see the subway doors close. I started to think a lot about destiny.

As a kid, I kissed my fingers or walked slowly to control the outcome of things, silently begging God—or whoever was listening—for a Slip 'n Slide, or sleepovers, or whatever else I wanted. As a newcomer to

New York City, I quickly learned to read the anatomical scribble of subway maps and to mimic the vacant stares of passersby, which guarded me against chatty creeps. But my newfound street smarts failed to soothe my mounting claustrophobia. That year, I observed two rats near a gas station in SoHo fighting over what appeared to be a piece of human feces, I watched a man die in my subway car, and I allowed Jonathan to hurt my feelings constantly. At the time, I was getting paid $2,000 a month at a consulting firm where my boss frequently wept while bombarding me with tales of his troubled marriage. Every day, I spotted and slogged through realities that rattled my romanticized versions of the city. My arms hurt from typing overtime, and occasionally I fell on my ass when the R train finally heaved into motion, and that hurt, too. More and more, I retreated into the tantalizing comfort of irrational patterns, where obsessives turn for a sense of order. Then I spent $150 I didn't have on a psychic I'd never met, and it changed my life forever.

I was walking home from work when Camilla the Clairvoyant stuck her head out the door of her storefront and yelled, "Hey, cutie! You got a funny family! Lots of siblings but not so many by blood—am I right?"

I halted, blinking. My parents had divorced when I was seventeen months old. My dad had remarried somebody with kids, then they had a kid, and then they divorced. My mom and my stepdad had babies, too. I was one of six but technically an only child.

Camilla stepped over the threshold, jamming a hip against the door to keep it open. Her gold crucifix glimmered against her purple dashiki. She was about forty years old, with thick, black, bobbed hair, and wearing more ankle bracelets than I had ever seen on one person. "Also you got some problems with, uh, what's-his-face?" She wrinkled her nose. "Starts with a J."

Jonathan.

The shock must have registered on my face, because she laughed. "Get in here," she said, waving.

As I climbed the steps to her office, my lower back ached and I found myself pondering the ergonomics of my home. After signing our shared lease five weeks prior, Jonathan had enthusiastically built all our furniture in one day using planks from the hardware store. Later, still beaming at my lover's industriousness, I realized with a frown that I couldn't reach the shelves he'd made. The benches he'd constructed were equally large—custom-fit to someone his size—and after enough time swinging my feet from those hard seats, bruises blossomed on my sit bones.

I settled gingerly onto one of the white patio chairs in Camilla's office, scooping my hair off the back of my sticky neck. It must have been more than eighty degrees outside, but it was stuffier inside, despite the fan sputtering weakly near our feet.

"It's not comfortable at home, is it?" she asked, reaching for her tarot cards. "It doesn't feel like yours."

I nodded. My sole contribution to the apartment was a world religions calendar I'd bought unused from Housing Works. As a kid growing up in the suburbs outside Milwaukee, I'd belonged to Fox Point Lutheran Church, but our family's attendance had been intermittent at best—and aside from knowing by heart a few undeniably catchy Jesus songs, most of what I understood about Christianity now came from that calendar. It was colorful, decorated with illustrations of everything from tribal masks to elaborately embroidered yarmulkes, and I wanted something hanging in our home that was mine.

"So what do you see?" I asked Camilla quietly as she nudged aside dusty candles and started slapping cards onto the table. The walls were painted purple, smothering any trace of the sunlight that managed to prick the mauve curtains covering the window.

"I see a lot," she said. "The cost of a session is $150, though." She looked up at me, waiting. The fan fluttering near our ankles wafted the smell of extinguished cigarettes and musky incense, and sent the clear beads hanging from the curtains clacking. Sweat trickled down my back.

"Do you take credit cards?"

"Of course."

I took a deep breath and wrestled a faded Visa from my wallet.

"You're stationary," she announced, as soon as I signed the receipt. "You're not moving like you should be moving. You're rusty." She smacked down more cards. "And don't let your boss confuse you," she added, shaking her head. "He's trouble—and who's this guy you like? It's not your boyfriend. I'm seeing an S somewhere—is there an S in his name? Not your boss, I mean a different guy."

I nodded again, now officially freaked out. Simon had been my college boyfriend and the first person I'd ever really loved. He and I met in a gay and lesbian fiction seminar where we were the only straight students. He thought I was a lesbian and I thought he was an F-to-M transgender person—he had this smooth, boyish face, except for one or two very long hairs, as if he had recently begun taking testosterone. The first time we locked eyes, my heart leapt, and I thought, *Well, I guess I have to explain queer theory to my dad—good thing we just learned about it in this class.* I'd never been so attracted to anyone in my life. We dated, off and on, for more than three years after that. I was wrong about the transgender thing.

"It isn't easy with Mr. S., is it?" Camilla asked.

I shrugged, but my stomach ached with butterflies—a sickly combination of desire and regret. The vacillating nature of my relationship with Simon had stemmed from the fact that I so often left him at the slightest hint of discord. I had no model for lasting relationships, or of people working through issues, so falling in love with him had been uncomfortable—a heady mix of euphoria and terror that he would inevitably leave.

After three years of quietly avoiding quarrels, I grew exhausted. I told him to forget about me and went out searching for something quieter, settling for someone who wished I were quieter. As far as I knew, Simon was dating someone else now, and my heart was swollen with sorry resignation. I had lost my chance, which, in my mind, was all the more reason to make things work with Jonathan.

"Your current relationship is empty," Camilla announced, reading my mind. "But don't worry about it, cutie, because there's true love in your future—I'd give it, say, three to four months. In the meantime, quit your job, quit your relationship. Life is not a conveyor belt—and there's a whole big rebirth in store for you if you'll just roll that dice." She shrugged. "I could do a palm reading for ten extra bucks. Gimme your hands."

I reached across the table.

That evening, Jonathan went to a bar and came home bleary-eyed. He climbed into bed beside me fully clothed and told me that my body nauseated him. Then he passed out.

I put down my book, baffled, and slunk out of the apartment, managing dry eyes until I felt sidewalk underneath my feet. Wailing in the moonlight like a lonesome wolf soothed my heartache in a way that snuffling in the shower never would—and besides that, in this town it was normal. I witnessed New Yorkers sobbing alfresco all the time—or at least I noticed it and then quickly averted my eyes, hoping others would do the same for me once it was my turn to fall apart.

So far the courtesy had always been reciprocal. But that night I cried so hard that even the chicken slaughterers locking up next door were visibly disturbed.

Later, as I lay in my sleeping bag under Jonathan's gigantic wooden table, picking sawdust off my nightgown and trying to get comfortable on the floor while he snored in the next room, Camilla's words ricocheted in my brain.

Quit everything.

As the sun rose, I tugged my world religions calendar from its nail and packed a duffel, hiding it inside my sweaty sleeping bag before heading out the door. I would gauge how I felt after work, I decided.

That afternoon, at lunch, my boss held another confessional with me about his wife, sharing secrets that embarrassed me on her behalf. As I munched my salad and tried to inoffensively ignore him, he looked up at me with watery eyes and asked for a hug. I put down my fork and gave him one.

"Oh, Kathleen," he said, breathing into my shoulder. "We have to be good."

I reddened. "What are you talking about?" I hissed. My blush felt like a rash, blistering my cheeks.

He squeezed harder, mistaking my embarrassment for coyness. "I used to think marriage meant loving one person," he said. "But it turns out, it's about not being allowed to love anybody else." He sighed into my hair. "I wish I'd met you sooner."

"I need to use the ladies' room," I announced, extricating myself from his clammy hands. Later in the day, I sent him a laboriously crafted email asking him to please stop sexually harassing me. But then again, the words echoed: "Quit everything." And a few minutes later, I quit my job and strode out of the office. I waited to break down until the smog hit my face.

Back in our empty apartment, I grabbed the duffel from my sleeping bag and scrawled a note on the back of our heating bill.

Look, I wrote. *I'm not trying to be melodramatic, I just didn't think I could face you. You're great, really. But we aren't, are we? It makes me sad.*

I paused.

Also I'm sorry this is in a note, I scribbled. *But I'm trying to be less indecisive, and I think part of being stronger maybe means practicing in the forums I'm comfortable with.*

I was running out of space.

I'll pay rent until you find a roommate, I concluded.

In dire situations, lonesomeness can feel the same as aloneness, and friendship can be hard to remember, much less quantify. That day, shuffling out of my former home, I reached for my phone and thumbed through my contacts—mostly to remind myself that people existed other than the ones with whom I'd been so preoccupied—and as I leaned against the wall of the Laundromat, swaddled in a comforting cloud of perfumed exhaust, I remembered that I actually knew a lot of people in Manhattan and Brooklyn. We'd hunched side by side on bar stools, and had regularly swapped group emails about cheap food or good happy hours, signed "xo." Like me, many of them were newcomers to the city and, as fellow initiates, our bonds had been contoured by culture shock that felt akin to hazing. Against the backdrop of a busy and congested metropolis, our every interaction had felt comparatively warm and intimate.

Now, scrolling through their numbers in my phonebook, the city suddenly felt less like an overcrowded fever dream, and more like a plethora of resources. I had friends in New York, and blessedly, most of them had couches.

For the rest of September, I paid close attention to that crumpled world religions calendar—jotting down interviews, circling drink dates. For money, I edited college essays for teenagers and after a few weeks, I got a job at another consulting firm.

Meanwhile, my ad hoc housing progressed from sleeping on friends' floors to snagging a month-long sublet in a Hasidic community near the Williamsburg Bridge. By November, Jonathan had found a new roommate, and I could afford to sign a lease. I painted my new room pale blue and bought a chair—overstuffed, this time, to comfortably cradle my butt. I could reach the cereal now. When I sat at the table, my feet touched the floor.

I started to wonder if terrible experiences might be necessary—a reference point by which to identify the good times through contrast. In New York, between the noise, the garbage, the smelly man on the subway and the guy behind you pressing his erection against your leg, your choices become the only uncrowded corners. The speed at which you walk, the interactions you invite by smiling or not—these decisions are sacred.

For me, bad experiences taught me to better encapsulate myself. After getting my own place, I started standing with my butt against the subway doors so I could read without ass grabbers getting in the way. I was warmer with my friends and colder (although not impolite) with my coworkers. Boundaries bred happiness for me.

Then Simon got in touch and asked if I wanted to meet him for a drink. I assumed he was going to tell me that he'd gotten engaged to that girl he was dating, and though my stomach sank, I had things I wanted to say to him. Sorry, for starters.

"How about December 28?" I asked, and circled it on the calendar.

A fter two bourbons, he still hadn't said anything about his girl-friend, which only made me more certain that he had one. Then I remembered our preconceived notions of each other back in gay and lesbian fiction. At the very least, it seemed like a good moment to apologize.

"Simon?" I asked, feeling wobbly with fear as he locked eyes with me. "I'm not trying to reinsert myself into your life or anything, but I need to tell you something."

He nodded, looking as if he were bracing himself for something horrible. I told him that I regretted the way I'd handled things. I said that I wished I had argued with him instead of running away, because as a result I had spent the last two years fantasizing about arguing with him. I explained that I would have settled for a screaming fight at any point over these past two years if it had just meant hearing his voice.

I was still talking when he grabbed my hand across the table.

"I thought you were engaged," he said.

Three years later, I was back in South Slope, en route to Camilla the Clairvoyant. Simon and I had recently gotten engaged and I wanted to thank her.

"Camilla!" I announced, beaming at her as she answered the door.

"Well, hey there, cutie." She smiled back at me. "Readings cost $150."

I dug in my purse. I hadn't come for advice, but I told myself it wouldn't hurt to hear what she had to say. It certainly hadn't hurt before.

As soon as I'd settled into the chair across from her and signed the credit card receipt, she got started.

"Work isn't going well," she said, eyeing the cards.

I grinned. "Actually, I really like my job—thanks to you, I—"

"Shh!" She flipped another card. "I'm seeing a red-haired man."

"You remember me, right?" My smile faded. "I came in a few years ago?"

Camilla shook her head. "That was my sister."

"But I recognize you—also, when I came in just now, you answered to the name Camilla—"

"Okay, hold up, cutie," she said, smirking. "I got you covered; you're going to find love soon—that's nice, right? Maybe as soon as next year . . . I'm seeing a J in his name."

"But I am in love. His name's Simon."

We stared at each other for what felt like an eternity.

"How about an aura reading for sixty more bucks?" she asked finally.

I'd like to say that I said "No"—that I ran into the street screaming, exclaiming to the world that the magic had been in me this entire time.

Instead I haggled the aura reading down to thirty bucks.

But this time I wasn't really listening.

CITY OF MUNDANE FANTASY

Elliott Kalan

On a pleasantly chilly autumn night, after a large Georgian dinner, walking with my best friend down the Coney Island Boardwalk while our wives talked fifteen or so paces behind, I couldn't help thinking, This is exactly the part in a Woody Allen movie where one of us would reveal to the other that we're cheating on our wife with our wife's best friend, fully aware that our wives can't hear us because they don't find out about the affair until later in the movie. And then the other would respond with disbelief but not really condemnation because the morality of the movie is a little weird and off-putting, and then make a joke, and then it would cut to a scene at the Guggenheim. But neither of us revealed anything like that. We were probably talking about movies.

I'm still not totally sure New York isn't just a movie. Even after fifteen years of near nonstop New Yorking, it still seems more filmic than real. Nothing I do in New York feels completely believable unless it reminds me of something I've seen someone do in New York in a movie. And even something as mundane as walking and talking becomes exciting when you see it in a movie. Especially something mundane like walking and talking.

New Yorkers are fascinated by movies, because movies are fascinated by New York. New York was where American movies were born, after all. Yes, history may tell us Thomas Edison's early studio was in New Jersey, but surely you, as I do, consider New Jersey a sort of surplus New Yorker–holding warehouse. Even after a hundred years in Los Angeles, New York is still the place the movies dream of. They pine for the hip, frosty girlfriend they abandoned for a pleasant if unexciting marriage to her sunnier, less mentally present sister coast.

As a result, movies are a young New Jersey boy's primer on New York and the methods of loving it. They were my invaluable education as I patiently waited, a surplus New Yorker, for someone to die and open up a spot for me there since God knows there was no place for me in New Jersey. Movies took me to my favorite of my childhood's two New Yorks. Not the New York I actually visited, the city of grandmothers and dinosaur-occupied museums, of zoos and scary homeless people you pretended not to see. I preferred the other New York, the New York I only saw in the movies. The City Where Grown-Ups Live.

The City Where Grown-Ups Live is the thrillingly everyday metropolis glimpsed around the edges of cinematic dreamery. I was first exposed to it in the magically titled *The Muppets Take Manhattan*. Magical to me not because of the "Muppet" part, but because of that beautiful, shining silver word, "Manhattan." The last word in the title because after you've read "Manhattan," any other word is an anticlimax. Hidden among the movie's many scenes of dancing animal puppets was a truly inspiring vision of adult normalcy. Kermit, the Muppets' frog vaudeville ringmaster, comes down with a case of cab crash–induced amnesia and is handed the identity of Phil, a New York ad exec. Phil does not perform on Broadway or hang out with a bear. Phil wears a suit and works in an office. Phil's days are spent attending meetings and having diner lunches with his coworkers. I wanted to be Phil.

What to the filmmakers was clearly a fate worse than death, the stifling of a unique spirit by the square establishment, was to young Elliott a dream to strive for. The message of numb conformity totally failed to reach me. All I could see was that Kermit went from naked frog to independent adult, autonomous professional, self-supported citizen. That was the magic of New York. Even an amphibian could become a grown-up. I didn't want to marry a pig and put on a show. I wanted a subway commute and a greasy spoon lunch hour. I wanted meetings around wooden tables. I wanted a desk with a phone on it. The return of Kermit's memory was tragic. He lost all those amazing ordinary things New Yorkers get to do!

Not that my vision of New York was a gray world of conformists and account execs. New York grown-ups seemed to have a constant awareness of the bizarre and strange inhabitants of its streets. Of the many things I loved in the nearly perfect *Gremlins 2: The New Batch* was the stream of pedestrians who refuse to register alarm or even look up as Dick Miller battles a flying bat-winged monster right on the sidewalk. I envied the powerful indifference of these grown-ups. I took this to mean that so many crazy things happen in New York, nothing could ever surprise or distract a grown-up New Yorker. "Another bat-monster fight? So what? Out of my way! I've got places to be!"

I wanted to be that adult so inured to the outrageous and insane that a hovering, reptiloid goblin wouldn't even catch my eye, let alone impress me enough to stop walking, head down, thinking about my lease or taxicabs or the Statue of Liberty, or whatever it is grown-up New Yorkers thought about on their way to the diners they were having lunch in.

And the most potent dose of New York mundanity by far was *Ghostbusters*, a movie yet to be given its due as a portrait of life in late-twentieth-century Manhattan. *Ghostbusters* was a major staple of my childhood. Before the age of thirteen I would estimate I watched it approximately one hundred million billion times. And each time I found myself entranced not by the beautifully tossed-off jokes of Bill Murray, nor by the majesty of the gargantuan Stay-Puft Marshmallow Man, nor even by the sheer terrifying evil of the snarling gargoyle demon dogs (though I did dream of riding one to school). I was drawn to the scene where Sigourney Weaver arrives at her building with an armful of brown grocery bags, briefly speaks to her neighbor in the hallway, and then unpacks her purchases in her kitchen.

Shortly after this, Weaver learns her apartment is haunted and there are monsters in her fridge. That was all fine and amusing. But when the movie was over what stayed with me were visions of high-rise living, tiny kitchens, and how the society of hallway neighbors could be simultaneously comforting and irritating. Having your own small space inside a larger network of human lives, a personal cell in a vast metropolitan hive, everyone scurrying their own way in and around each other to get to their tiny pockets of privacy and quiet. As a child I knew this was how I wanted to live. The New York grown-up way.

Ghostbusters might be where I first met a sacred and potent fetish of New York living: the late-night Chinese takeout work dinner. Though here it appears in diluted, impure form, since the Chinese takeout is enjoyed at a renovated firehouse they also live in and not at an office desk by a tie-knot-loosened employee. But still, all the possibilities and promises of grown-up living were represented by that strangely not-quite-square white cardboard box with the thin metal handle. That perfectly compact package of ethnic food, compressed like the city's adults themselves into a small yet private and anonymous compartment. Its use as after-hours workplace sustenance became the subject of innumerable daydreams.

What kind of job, I wondered, will I be doing someday that requires me to stay so late that I must call someone to box up some noodles and deliver them directly to me? How many years will pass before I become such an expert wielder of those tapered sticks that I can use them to eat directly out of the box? In my mind, children ate with fork and knife off a plate. Adults were too busy to empty out their cartons of food and switch between two different utensils. They had work to do. New York work. At New York night. The most exciting kind of night.

The Chinese takeout container, chopsticks planted firmly like the flag of the Grown-Up nation, held the everyday, ordinary moments of a New Yorker: The haunted apartment door closing behind you so you can put down your groceries. The silent shuffling of chairs as you and your fellow frog ad execs get up from a meeting. The white noise of the blurry city around you as you bull through the streets, head down, ignoring the gremlins in the air.

Any vision of New York that failed to include these peeks of the mundane was useless to me. The less dull the characters' day was, the more bored I got. The real disappointment of a movie like *Friday the 13th Part VIII: Jason Takes Manhattan* wasn't the lame scares, the irritating characters, or the fact that Jason doesn't actually get to Manhattan until most of the movie is over. It's that Jason didn't end his day of murdering teenagers by stopping at the bodega for toilet paper and cat food, picking up moo goo gai pan for dinner, and eating it at his tiny apartment's even tinier kitchen table while watching the local news on WPIX.

The weird thing is I never wanted to be a New York child. That seemed too difficult and too dangerous. I never had the skills or wits to charm my way into shelter and food, *Home Alone 2*–style. So I bided my time and at seventeen enrolled in NYU, where I could live the life of a grown-up in training, less a college student than a New Yorker whose day job was going to college. Eager to achieve full grown-up–hood, I rushed through the core curriculum like a number 2 express train barreling straight from Fourteenth Street to Seventy-Second with the bare minimum of stops in between.

Then, success! Within a few years I was experiencing the very things I'd fantasized about as a child. I wore a tie to a job. I commuted to work, keeping my head down and ignoring the people around me. I went home to my tiny apartment and put away my groceries in my tinier kitchen. And every now and then I even got to stay late at work eating Chinese takeout food.

And you know what? It sucked. Sure, I enjoyed the brief moment when the Chinese food entered my mouth. But only as an adult did I realize that working late was a drag, bringing home groceries was a pain, and New Yorkers ignore the city around them because city transit is a soul-crushing experience. Being a grown-up in New York is often extremely exciting. But despite what I thought as a boy, not the boring parts. That's why everyone calls them the boring parts. Because they're boring.

Yet still, I can't completely shake the glow of wonder about it. When I watch movies set in New York, I still feel a tingle of hope that some-day I may get to live in that place and be one of those people. And that hope persists long after I remind myself that I *do* live in that place and I'm *already* one of those people. The mundane fantasy of this city has entrenched itself in my soul, and no amount of reality can dislodge it. If I'm being kind to myself, I'd say this was because I've maintained a sense of childlike wonder. But as a New Yorker I'm essentially a cynic, so instead I'll chalk it up to denial.

But let's play devil's advocate and say my mundane fantasy of the City Where Grown-Ups Live is special. That it possesses a quality no other fantasies can lay claim to: I've achieved them. The fantasies the movies peddled to me, on the other hand—a world of ghosts, grem-lins, and musical cloth animals—are not only unachievable, they're totally impossible. Why should I settle for a fantasy I can never see come to life when I can live my fantasies every single day? My mun-dane dreams of New York were far healthier, better, more emotionally stable dreams than anything Hollywood could come up with—and so powerful, Hollywood couldn't stop them from leaking through the fabric of their made-up nonsense.

I believe everyday New York fantasies are better than fantastical New York fantasies. And we all believe, because it's true, that New York is the greatest place on earth. And so ipso facto, I must conclude logically and mathematically that the dull, ordinary dreams of my childhood were the best of all possible dreams. After all, they're the only dreams guaranteed to become a reality.

SF → NYC

Isaac Fitzgerald

The first time I considered moving to New York City I was fresh out of college and there was a job on the table: "I know a guy we could deal cocaine for," my buddy Pete said.

It was tempting. I'd spent the whole summer working on a paint maintenance crew on an island off the coast of New Hampshire, and the idea of moving to the largest city in the country had its appeal. Not to mention that I'd always thought I'd be good at dealing cocaine.

My other option was to work for little money on a long-shot congressional campaign in Pennsylvania's Eighth District. Much to the relief of pretty much everyone I knew, that's what I ended up doing. The candidate was Patrick Murphy, an Iraq war vet who would eventually win, become the youngest Democrat on the Hill, and help get rid of Don't Ask, Don't Tell, only to be voted out again in 2010.

But I wouldn't be there for any of that. After six months on the campaign trail, sleeping in suits and living in an unheated, unfinished room built out of crumbling drywall on a diet of scotch to help me fall asleep, I, with a fresh degree in political science and episodes of *The West Wing* bouncing around in my head, realized that I had made a terrible four-year-long mistake. Politics wasn't for me.

Luckily I had an escape route. I'd met a girl while painting all those buildings in New Hampshire—a girl who had just moved to San Francisco. Like so many of us who don't know what to do with ourselves, I chased a relationship. While all my friends on the East Coast were moving to New York City, I moved three thousand miles away. California was totally unfamiliar.

My life had been East Coast all the way, from Boston to Philadelphia to Washington, DC. But moving to the West Coast gave me something staying back east didn't: much-needed distance from my childhood. I had a history with my parents, as any of us who have parents do. A history of a combative household filled with explosive arguments and estranged silence. My parents were married when they had me, just to different people. Their lives weren't easy. Not enough money or trust, too many tough situations with no way to win. We lived poor in Boston at a halfway house for low-income families run by the Catholic Worker, and then in North Central Massachusetts, white and rural and impoverished.

In North Central Massachusetts, my parents began to reconcile. But I was still a child and unable to understand the difficulties that they had faced. Angry and resentful, I turned to the distractions available to me in backwoods Massachusetts—riding around in trucks, consuming beer and terribly stepped-on drugs in deserted forests and quarries. As the wounds between my parents healed, I withdrew from them, unable to forgive them for being human.

San Francisco was beautiful and new and strange, but my bad habits made the trip with me. A year after I arrived, the girl moved back east to get away from our relationship, which was really more of a drinking partnership at that point. She left, but I stayed, bottle in hand.

I lived in a one-bedroom apartment that I shared with three people, where mice ran across the kitchen table while you were eating like you weren't even there and pigeons nested in the walls. I waited tables at Buca di Beppo (which was like Olive Garden but worse), slung beers at old, punk-encrusted bars, and at one point was the world's worst sushi chef. At five a.m. every morning, I got up to make rolls that I would then drive to different tech campuses—Google, LinkedIn, Facebook—stocking their snack refrigerators with the hard-rolled fruits of my labor from a blue beer cooler. In my uniform of a black T-shirt and ripped jeans, and reeking of fish, I'd drag the cooler through brightly lit offices where everything matched except me, as I skulked past beautiful, well-dressed kids my own age having loud sex on the tops of piles of money. At least that's how I remember it.

The years passed, and crappy jobs turned into less crappy jobs, as they tend to if you stay in one place long enough. Bouncing turned into barbacking turned into a few shifts bartending turned into a trip running medical supplies illegally into Burma out of Thailand turned into a job for a news website that actually had a steady paycheck and health insurance. I quit after a year because a friend offered me an opportunity that was too good to pass up: taking a fifty percent pay cut and absolutely no insurance whatsoever to help him with his new online arts and culture magazine called The Rumpus. But, hey. Talking about books online might be a meager living, but it was still a living. And it was *talking about books online.*

As a child I had always loved books but never had a clue about how they were made. For the first time, surrounded by the amazing artists and writers of the Bay Area, I was thriving in a job that I actually enjoyed. I stopped drinking tequila in the morning (for the most part) and eventually moved into an incredible, illegally subletted, way-too-grown-up-for-me rent-controlled studio that I had all to myself. The city, which initially seemed to reject my very presence, slowly began to tolerate me, and then—it felt like—champion me. And in turn I championed her. "Look, look," I would say, grabbing everyone who would listen, "look at this, the most beautiful city in the world. This is my home."

Then my new job began bringing me east, more and more. My parents and I started getting in touch more often. When I first got to San Francisco, I would call every week on Sunday, like the lapsed Catholic I was. In return, they would never visit. We maintained that schedule for years, until my first piece of writing was published: an essay about letting a woman fuck me in the ass with a strap-on. My father didn't come to the phone for six months, although my mother and I still spoke. Then, one Sunday, my father picked up the line. We talked baseball, as one does when talking about feelings is too harrowing to consider. Sunday by Sunday, despite the distance, we grew closer. The calls turned into one visit, then two. My parents had moved, and our old home was behind us. The things I held against them, the things they held against themselves, seemed to soften with age. Instead of avoiding them when I was in New York on business, I invited them into the city for dinner.

After eight years of living in San Francisco and fighting to carve out a life of my own far away from my childhood home, I moved back to the East Coast. The decision came quickly. My half brother, from my mother's previous marriage, was struggling to start a new family. He and his wife had suffered a devastating miscarriage on Christmas Day the previous year, a Christmas I wasn't there for, and they'd been trying to get pregnant again ever since.

We spoke on the phone often. He'd describe fertility tests and drugs I couldn't pronounce, procedures and endless appointments with doctors nearly as numerous as the miles that stood between the Atlantic and the Pacific. They lived on the New Hampshire coast, near where I'd painted those houses and met that woman who brought me west. I felt useless, wearing my armor of three thousand miles.

When he told me that he and his wife had finally succeeded— that they would be starting a family in the summer—I realized that I wanted to be there. That I didn't want distance to be a part of our family's next steps. My half sister, from my father's previous marriage, lived in New York City. She didn't know a guy I could deal cocaine for, but she would be happy to share the city with me and even help me find a place to live.

I moved in December. The winter was the harshest that it had been in years, or so people would say as they saw me shiver through the drifts of snow, longing for the California sun. Like San Francisco, New York did not welcome me with open arms. Why should it? New York is just a place. A city. It has no feelings toward me one way or the other.

When I got to New York, I was the age my parents were when they had met and had me. What does anyone know about living life at thirty? About as much as I knew about the subway, I'd have said, as I took the wrong trains, missed my stops, and tried to figure out if Coney Island was ever the right direction to go in.

I saw my parents more in four months than I had in the past eight years. All I had to do was walk outside my apartment and money would disappear from my pockets. I stepped into every deceptively shallow-looking monster slush puddle that seasoned New Yorkers knew to avoid. I was anxious, feeling as though the entire eastern seaboard bore down on my shoulders, trying to push me underground.

The thing about missing eight winters, though, is that you forget that you also missed eight springs. Now, the sun is here. I no longer hide underground, crowded into subway cars that I worry I'll never get used to. Riding my bicycle over the Manhattan Bridge, I see the city, instead of scuttling beneath it. And it is *beautiful*. Parks. Markets. Blossoms. People. Dresses. Pavement. This city is alive and full of wonder and I am just one lost person in it, but I wouldn't want to be lost anywhere else. That's the flip side to leaving a city that made me feel cozy and comfortable and loved: I get to be lost. I have an entire expanse of concrete to explore, to learn about, to appreciate. And to hell with concrete—I hear there's a beach, even. I look forward to meeting the Rockaways, and perfect summer midnights and bitching about the heat and the smell of baked garbage. I look forward to meeting all the joys and challenges of a new city remade for a new season. My brother's daughter will be born this summer. I look forward to meeting her too.

PUBLISHING: A LIKE STORY

Maris Kreizman

There was a time in the predigital age, a time before e-readers and tablets and mobile phone apps, when taking an entry-level publishing job was like signing on to fight a war against paper. Back in the days when book publishers killed trees and prospective authors' dreams with equal abandon, there would be territory battles for access to that one Xerox machine on the eleventh floor that jammed less frequently than the other ones. There were "It's not you, it's me" letters to be written and mailed back to literary agents along with scads of rejected book proposals. There were faxes to be sent and received, legal-size contracts to be filed, and pink perforated phone messages to be recorded and disbursed. There were copyedits to shepherd, reams of marked-up pages that smelled of coffee or whiskey or baby vomit, depending on the current life stages of both author and editor. There was so much mail. There were piles upon piles of manuscript pages to be collated and read and evaluated beneath unforgiving fluorescent lights, and ensuing headaches caused by eye strain and recycled air and too much Diet Coke.

I grew up in the suburbs of New Jersey, the area Springsteen sang so many songs about leaving, but I never felt an urgency to flee my hometown. I certainly never had my heart set on becoming a New Yorker. It was those damn headaches that felt like they were my birthright. Like most New Yorkers I know, I am happiest when things are awful. I find joy in seeking out wonderful ways to be miserable, so it only made sense that I was drawn to the glamorous world of book publishing. Those headaches, and all the crazy hours and adorable little paychecks that accompanied them, made me feel alive. I loved those headaches. I was privileged—literally—to be able to experience those headaches (thanks for the safety net, Mom and Dad!). Those headaches meant that I had found my place in the world, alongside equally masochistic and idealistic people who loved to read as much as I did and who were prepared to sacrifice emotional and financial stability in order to turn their love of reading into a career. In other words, my colleagues were as crazy as I was, in the best possible way.

I blame George Plimpton. I met him at the very first swanky publishing party I ever attended, at a townhouse on the Upper East Side. I was drinking wine that didn't come from a box and was feeling very optimistic about my future prospects. And then there he was, the New York literary legend. I bravely approached Mr. Plimpton to introduce myself, and he said he was delighted to meet me, and perhaps he was more focused on checking out my breasts than on our conversation. Talking to him was so exciting! Degrading too, of course, but also very exciting. Just like the publishing industry!

I blame Chloë Sevigny too. I look back now on *The Last Days of Disco* and realize that the film finds many uncomfy parallels between an outmoded style of music and nightlife and the book publishing industry. Dinosaurs, both. But gosh, Chloë made it all look so fun and stylish.

I especially blame Margaret Atwood and Lorrie Moore and Susan Sontag and Charles freaking Dickens. I blame Toni Morrison and

Roald Dahl and all the uncelebrated ghostwriters known collectively as "Francine Pascal" for the Sweet Valley High series. And yes, I blame Joan Didion. It was the idea of eventually working with writers like those that made me feel okay about the countless hours I spent, in the meantime, editing books that weren't uniformly thrilling. I relished the thankless coordinating I did for ghostwritten celebrity tell-alls, and I didn't mind babysitting a bunch of self-help authors, who were notoriously the least self-actualized nutcases on the planet. Those books were the reality TV shows of the book biz, the ones that would appeal to the masses and thereby finance the riskier, more thought-provoking books that I might one day publish to great acclaim. Because there was always the chance that somewhere buried in the slush pile, I'd find . . . blah blah blah. You get it, no need for me to fill in the details. Let's just say I had visions of National Book Awards, lifelong friendships with authors I'd edited, and stimulating parties filled with people who'd engage in water-cooler talk about a newly published literary novel like it was the latest greatest show on HBO. I remember that when I acquired my first book as an assistant editor—a subversively funny story collection by an up-and-coming superstar—I received a congratulatory email from a senior editor I'd been crushing on. I think I skipped down Sixth Avenue that day.

I chose to make a life for myself in the epicenter of the book publishing world, the one place in the United States where performing menial tasks every day ultimately gave me a great sense of purpose. By choosing publishing, I also chose New York City. I chose to share a railroad-style apartment with three other women, scurrying like a mouse through our connected rooms alongside the actual mice that were scurrying through them. I chose to live in a location where mundane items became unimaginable luxuries: a dishwasher, a porch, a yard, a car, a washer/dryer in one's home. A supermarket. A Target where the women's apparel hasn't been thoroughly picked over. I chose summers that smelled of hot garbage and winters so icy that it was barely possible to slink over to the corner bodega without falling on your ass numerous times.

But New York was like the free bookshelf by the ladies' room at the office: there was a lot of unwanted crap stacked on those shelves, but there was often a gem or two to be found if you were motivated enough to dig around. There were endless possibilities. Dinner might be a rubber-banded container from the deli across the street where the entire salad bar was fifty percent off after five p.m., but then dessert could be a glass of champagne at a debut novelist's launch party. An acrid-smelling misogynist could proselytize about the impropriety of your attire on the subway, but the train itself would be speeding toward some moment of transcendent beauty, even if it was just a publishing assistant sing-along at some Koreatown karaoke bar.

The problem with choosing an identity and a lifestyle that's tied to a particular profession is, of course, that you must rely on job security for a sense of self-worth. In 2008 I left the corporation where I'd slowly but surely been making a name for myself for five years in order to take a job at a smaller publisher where ideally I'd have more authority—or at least fewer phones to answer. Four months into the job, my division was sold, and I lost my job. It was the worst breakup I'd ever experienced. I was a spurned lover, frantically trying to figure out what was left of me if my beloved had rejected me. What made me *me* if I wasn't a book editor? Being unemployed in New York City in the springtime should've been somewhat enjoyable. The city was alive and I had the time to take it all in! I was receiving unemployment checks, after all, and poverty wasn't imminent. But that season felt like one long panic attack, made worse by the fact that I felt overwhelmingly stressed about not being able to just relax and enjoy myself. This, as many neurotic and/or driven people know, is a vicious cycle.

After a string of desperate dates (informational interviews, really—

it turned out my layoff coincided with an economic crisis that led to mass consolidation in the publishing world), I found a vaguely book-related position at a startup and I snapped it up. I spent years at that damn job, watching from afar as former contemporaries climbed their respective corporate ladders and became forces in the publishing field. I was jealous and frustrated, and so, as many others have done before and will continue to do, I took to the Internet.

I had spent years trying to help others find their own distinctive voices, and I was amazed to find that I could help myself in the same way. It turned out I didn't need stationery or a corporate card or a fancy job title in order to take part in New York book culture. And I didn't need a book deal in order to be a writer. I didn't even need to consider myself to be a *writer* in order to be a writer. "Serious" writerly types might bemoan the detrimental effect that social media have on productivity or creativity, but one of the most rewarding things I've ever done was to start a silly Tumblr blog called *Slaughterhouse 90210* on a whim. I was bored at work and a friend suggested that I create a blog featuring some of my favorite quotes from literature—I had thousands. But quotes alone weren't fun. I realized that if I juxtaposed quotes from books I loved with images from TV shows, my blog posts would be entertaining and provide unique commentary.

Slaughterhouse 90210 was singularly *mine*. I could never be fired from it! My blog gave me a platform to become a writer and critic and performer, encouraged by the literary community I found on Tumblr. I was inspired by all my newfound Bookternet friends—readers, writers, bloggers, booksellers, publishing world types, and fellow refugees. You certainly didn't have to live in New York City to take part in the discussion. But it sure was fun getting to know some of these new friends in real life. There are an abundance in this city.

A fundamental tenet of society at large is that book readings are supposed to be boring. Why would anyone want to spend an evening listening to some pretentious twerp drone on and on? How many tiny plastic cups of cheap chardonnay would one have to drink not to mind when a creep in the back row asks the reader intensive questions about the creative process? Or if he has more of a comment than a question? One of the most magical things about New York is that readings are not boring here. On any given night, there are at least three or four literary events taking place in New York, and thanks to great curation and a high level of passion among event planners, at least two or three of them will be delightful. I can walk into any one of an amazing collection of local bookstores and know that I'll be inspired and entertained, and that I'll have a friend or two in the audience. I love that. As highly esteemed experts have been saying for many years, book publishing is undergoing many technological shifts. It's in a constant state of flux. But literary *culture*, especially in New York City, is alive and well and essential.

Life is sometimes shitty. I don't ascribe the shittiness of life to New York, maybe because I don't really know any other way of adult life, so I have little to compare it to. I ascribe my bouts of unhappiness to being a person who sometimes has difficulty relaxing and taking it all in. Betrayals and heartache and injustices take place everywhere, and loneliness is pervasive. But reading and being on the Internet and living in New York City are simultaneously solitary and intensely social activities. Somehow sitting on the couch in my apartment in Greenpoint, all alone with a book, I feel surrounded by friends.

ESB

Rachel Syme

This is the first time I refer to the Empire State Building as my boyfriend: I am twelve years old. I am writing in my diary, staring out of a second-story bay window at the base of a ten-thousand-foot peak that looms over my adobe house in Albuquerque, New Mexico. "Mountains are tall but skyscrapers are taller," I write. I am wrong, of course—even the adobe house, at seven thousand feet above sea level, is already perched six times as high above sea level as the mooring mast atop the Empire State—but I need to maintain the fantasy of a loftier place, soaring and immense, the antithesis of the overbaked flatness of my hometown. I scribble "Me + ESB = Love," drawing a heart around the letters, as if carving them into a tree.

Later that year, I visit New York for the first time, where I bunk with a towheaded bully from my junior high chorus in the Hotel Edison. Our room has stained carpets and creaky beds that wheeze dust when bounced on. We are there on a field trip, to sing standards from the American songbook on Carnegie Hall's main stage, and I have never experienced anything so grand. Still, I quietly save up my elation for the observation deck of the building I had been writing love letters to for years, the apex of the place I might someday belong to, that might someday belong to me. When we reach the top, I break off from the group of whooping tweens to peer out over the edge and out across the city by myself: my first communion. I am the smallest person in my class, the runt, the easy punch line. But the building doesn't mock my size, it bolsters me. It wants me to feel as tall as it is. "I love you, I love you, I love you," I whisper to the tower (always my deepest desires in threes, a superstitious child's ritual). Somewhere I hear a chaperone calling my name, and I follow an instinct: I kiss the cold metal of the railing, and I promise to return.

Sophomore year of college, Palo Alto, California, where my father went. Where we all thought I might be happy reading classics in the sun. But I hate the West Coast. I can't adapt to the fog, the aquatic currents that chill the bones day and night, the parties that seem to happen only around bonfires and barbecue pits. I spend much of that year hiding out in my room, watching and rewatching an eight-part documentary about the history of New York City. I memorize the names. Boss Tweed. Al Smith. Fiorello LaGuardia. Frederick Law Olmsted. Emma Lazarus.

And John Jakob Raskob: a name in three parts. I know I owe him a great deal.

Raskob worked his way up from a secretary for entrepreneur and GM manager Pierre S. du Pont to a multimillionaire in the position to dream up the Empire State Building by 1930, placing a pencil in front of architect William Lamb and asking, "Bill, how high can you make it so that it won't fall down?" His only goal was to beat the height of the two other major towers going up (40 Wall and Chrysler), pushing an exhausted team to erect 103 stories in only fifteen short months. Hubris was never a problem for Raskob, but timing was. Just two months before the stock market crashed, he gave an interview in *Ladies'*

Home Journal saying that "everybody ought to be rich." He opposed the New Deal just as it became the nation's saving grace. When the tower opened in 1931, far from major transportation hubs and in the midst of an economic nightmare, its deck thrilled visitors, but it could never attract tenants and would not turn a profit for twenty years. Locals called it the "Empty State Building" under their breath.

What Raskob had built was ghostly inside, but tremendous to behold, its lights a surrogate constellation for city dwellers who had no stars of their own. "Here is our poetry," Ezra Pound wrote in 1913, when the first skyscrapers surged into the atmosphere. "For we have pulled the stars down to our will."

I learn that quote from the documentary too, and I repeat it, seething. California's sky is full of stars and I don't feel tall enough yet to lasso them. Like Raskob, I find myself racing for height, the glory and the folly of it. I'm ready to get above myself, over my own head.

The day after I graduate, I get on a plane to New York City. I say goodbye to no one. I have a twin bed waiting but no other plan, other than to collect the earlier self I'd left on the observation deck and take her with me. I smile so hard on the plane when the outline of the city comes into view that the woman next to me asks me if I am on the way to see my boyfriend. I tell her yes.

I am twenty-four and meeting a man for a late dinner at Florent, the twenty-four-hour diner on an oily cobblestone street near the Hudson River. A drag queen stands on the chrome bar, shouting orders for fries back toward the kitchen. Four years later, the diner will close and become a designer boutique, along with all the other businesses in the neighborhood, an outdoor promenade for the kind of wealthy who don't balk at spending $350 on a pair of cashmere socks. But that night, I order steak frites and play footsie underneath the bar with the musician, seven years my senior and a fixture in New York. I have just been made a junior editor at a new glossy magazine that plans to poke holes in the zeitgeist with devastating puns, and I then consider it a dramatic rise from my beginnings as fact-checker (and de facto coffee delivery service) at a more storied publication. I feel tall. Inside Florent, I feel even taller, as the musician takes my hand.

Here is the story of the musician: He went searching for me. He saw my face in a photograph and reposted it on his website, asking the ether to match a name to this girl, a mystery for the public with me as the answer. I woke up blurry the next morning to dozens of hysterical messages from strangers, pleading with me to respond. I knew exactly who he was and what I had to do. I should have felt intimidated or leery or even scared, but I was calm. Everything was always happening in New York, and always at the same time. Shock would be inappropriate. I was a craver of height, anything to build another story. I put a single post on my own site, "Yes, that's me," and left my email. In an hour, a note came in with the subject line "So you are real." Three months later, we are ordering milkshakes from a man in heels.

Some people stare at us in Florent, but mostly they leave us alone. I realize in the diner that I am starting to love the willful ignorance of New Yorkers, the ability to look at the epic and beautiful and quickly put it into context. It's a skill that comes from the skyline; we see something that magnificent every day and somehow go on living. A backdrop like that will dominate you unless you learn to become a part of it, and that's what New Yorkers do. Become towers.

The musician and I never eat steaks together again. He becomes a vegan and moves west. He even sells his apartment, which has a small sliver of a view of the Empire State Building from the bedroom window. Later, he tells me that the view is what he misses most.

. . .

Summer, twenty-seven years old. I am crying and walking up Fifth Avenue wearing five-inch heels that I had bought at Bergdorf Goodman just a week before, in better times. The building looming over me feels like the closest approximation of a north star, which is useful as I am completely lost. I have just left my job at a cultural website for good due to a departmental redundancy, a term that was supposed to soften the blow but makes me feel erased. My partner of the last two years, a gentle, doe-eyed East Coast intellectual who uses too many words to say how he feels and made me love him for it, has finally run out of words other than goodbye. This is the first time I ever seriously contemplate leaving New York City. I live in South Brooklyn, in a crumbling but cheap apartment that looks out over Atlantic Avenue, where lovers often quarrel in the street and threaten to hit one another. The city feels mean and small, and I feel smaller in it. At some point that summer, a mouse crawls into my bathtub to die, and it's the final sign. I take a job in another city, two hours away by train, and though I know I am making a mistake even before the Vermonter leaves Penn Station, I promise to cut my losses. I start to delete the intellectual's number on my phone, realizing that in the place of his photograph in my contacts list I have put a picture of the Empire State Building glowing red. I wonder if I took the picture on Valentine's Day or Christmas. He liked to joke that the photo was a sign of his virility. He made that joke too much.

Returning to New York, triumphant, jubilant, twenty-eight. I only lasted ten months in the new city. I broke my promise to stop looking back and took the train into Penn Station every single weekend, squatting in my old apartment until the landlord caught on. I was so homesick that I finally put a book proposal together after so many years of sitting on it, and selling it became my ticket home. When people ask me if they should leave New York, I tell them only if they are using it as an opportunity to ride back in on a float.

You have to live where you feel tall.

I move into a sunny one-bedroom in Greenpoint, a neighborhood right across the water from Thirty-Fourth Street, and I can see the mooring mast from my front stoop. I say good morning and good night to it, and hello throughout the day. Me + ESB = Love. I start to build myself up again. I write inside the public library, passing through the marble lions in the mornings. I start to buy silk kimonos and wear them around my apartment like I'd always imagined I might. I begin to buy fresh flowers on my walks and put them everywhere. I frequent dress shops on the Upper West Side where stylish octogenarian eccentrics pick out clothes for me to wear. "You're not dressing for the grave," one tells me, adjusting a caftan that makes me feel like hosting a cocktail hour. "You will never be this young again."

I learn to change my appearance like the Empire changes colors, picking out a character for the day—turbans, false eyelashes, fur stoles, a leather bomber, a flower crown, vintage snakeskin pumps. The city encourages expansiveness. I feel alive again in New York, but I also know that I am living less and less in the New York that is, and more in the New York that was—John Jakob Raskob's New York, a time of blanket optimism and martinis in hotel bars. I try to ignore the fact that Manhattan has become less and less of a place for old eccentrics who want to dress someone up. I try to ignore the condo going up on a corner where I remember laughing with a friend so hard that I fell over and cut my lip, or the chain taking over the Mexican restaurant where I used to pass sections of the Sunday paper back and forth with a man I loved. After a while we could do it without looking up. I try to ignore how much I miss Florent, and I may always miss the girl I was when it was still there. My tower is still standing, though now it has a new owner, who tries too hard, putting on a flashing laser light show. Hubris again. I try to ignore that too.

Today. Thirty years old. I sometimes think about leaving New York and returning to the mountains. Many of my friends have moved away or are in the process of doing so. They cannot afford the rent, and the businesses they love are shuttering. I too don't recognize the young people downtown, members of a tribe I cannot join. I wonder if they love that building like I do. I wonder if they know who made it. It's the only question I ever want to ask them.

But I find it almost impossible to leave it behind, that lighthouse, my first love. I almost move to Los Angeles every year, but I never wrote love letters to it. I never learned its founders' names.

You have to keep living where you feel tall. You have to keep living in the place where people search for you and find you.

As a friend was moving away, he told me that he wanted to go somewhere where he can still build things. "What," he asked, "am I *building* in New York?" I didn't know what to tell him then, but this is what I would tell him now: in New York, you are demanded to build yourself. The environment calls for it. You build on pure speculation, a foundation up from the salty bedrock built upon something that was there before, as many stories high as you want to go, as fast as you can get there. It is possible to fail, possible to outpace yourself, to not turn a profit, to remain empty inside with your lights still blazing for show. But when it works, what you build becomes a beacon. Here is our poetry. Here are the stars bending to our will. Here we are touching them.

THE STUDIED KNOWLEDGEABILITY OF THE NATIVE NEW YORKER

Amy Sohn

In the summer of 1995, after graduating from Brown, I reinstalled myself in my childhood bedroom in Brooklyn Heights to save money and try to get a job. Surrounded by my old Billy Joel albums, high school textbooks, and the yellow carpet stain from a mustache-bleaching accident at fourteen, I felt like I was a teenager all over again. And yet there was no shame in this. I was not a loser but a pragmatist.

For the native New Yorker, the decision to live in the city as an adult springs not from reckless bravery but thrift. This was a temporary plan, designed to get me on my feet. I signed up with a temp agency, re-signed with my old acting agent (I had done a lot of theater as a child), and began going on auditions. I told everyone I was a temptress—a temp and an actress.

I had an active, fun social life; one thing native New Yorkers need not worry about is making new friends. I went to bars, films, and dinners with high school and camp pals, most of them also living with their parents.

That fall, I got a call from Noah, a friend I had met through the very small and insular world of progressive college–age Jews. A native of

Massachusetts, Noah was in grad school in the city. "My sister Katherine just moved to Hell's Kitchen," he said, "and she's looking to meet new people. Why don't we all go to dinner?"

We met in the Village and I liked Katherine immediately. She had long dark hair and blue eyes, and she was bright, sarcastic, and a little shy. She laughed easily and though she smoked Camel Lights and wore motorcycle boots, there was something vulnerable about her. She was sharing an apartment with two roommates and caring for a handicapped man while interning for no pay at a magazine.

A few days later she called me and we began getting together a couple of times a week for coffee, dinner, or drinks. We often went to the Big Cup, a gay-friendly café in Chelsea, where we would talk explicitly about our sexual histories while surrounded by gay men who had no interest in eavesdropping. After I booked a play in Tribeca, we would hang out at the Knitting Factory on Leonard Street, or the old Knitting Factory on East Houston Street (now Botanica). I took her to Sophie's in the East Village, where I had drunk illegally in high school. I took her to Max Fish, Luna Lounge, Mercury Lounge, and the Brooklyn Inn in Boerum Hill, where Paul Auster had recently shot a movie starring Harvey Keitel.

Feeling that Noah wanted me to take good care of Katherine, I shared with her all my New York insider tips: First Avenue and Allen Street are the same thing, you have to know which part of the train to get on in if you want to avoid a long walk at your destination, and if you need to orient yourself, just look for the Twin Towers (south).

Though we were both dating actively, that took up only so many hours per week. The rest we spent with each other. She soon found a rent-controlled apartment in the East Village and became a regular at bars like the International and Big Bar, which wasn't big. At that time in New York City if you were young and single, the thought of staying home was anathema. The only thing at home was *Ally McBeal*.

Out meant bars, live music, alternative comedy, literary readings, and sex. There was a Molson Ice commercial featuring grungy-looking twenty-somethings, and in the voiceover, John Lurie growled, "Maybe I'll go to a city that never sleeps and maybe I'll put it to bed. What are you going to do?" We were all taking that question very much to heart.

Katherine and I would sit at one of our haunts—she drinking Jameson, me whiskey sours—and talk about boys. We covered first loves, loss of virginity, most painful breakups. She was less promiscuous and more orgasmic. She was better at smoking, I was better at pool.

I welcomed her to my parents' apartment for dinner, where she endured my father's quizzing about her life goals. Once she came for the weekend to their house in the Berkshires. We went downhill skiing and I envied her sleek style. At night she smoked on the downstairs porch while I worried they would smell it, and we slept side by side on a fold-out couch, whispering confidences. Though our relationship was never sexual, the intimacy I felt with her was romantic. I had struggled in college to form meaningful, intense bonds with women because I was so busy with dysfunctional relationships. My friendship with Katherine felt like a correction for that, and it was made richer by the fact that we were young adults with dreams—she wanted to be a short-story writer, I wanted to make it in theater.

A few times I introduced her to guys I had dated and she would sleep with them. Sometimes she would date them for a few months, longer than I had been able to. I never told her I was jealous. I was a native New Yorker, and native New Yorkers are generous with ex-lovers, and they understand that no one owns anyone. Once, we were at Veselka with an art-gallery assistant, a cute male friend of hers with a Paul Rudd vibe. He looked from her to me and said, "You two approach men completely differently. Katherine attracts men like this"—he slumped in his seat, lowered his eyelids and chin, and made bedroom eyes—"and Amy approaches them like this"—he opened his eyes and mouth, like in yoga class when you growl like a lion. It was true; she was quiet, contained, seductive. I met cute boys and did magic tricks, cursed, propositioned. My fear was that her method was more successful than mine, that guys liked her more because she knew how to be a little bit mean to them. I was never mean to guys because I wanted them all to love me.

One rainy Sunday night, around eleven, while walking near Borough Hall toward the Brooklyn Inn, Katherine and I were mugged by two teenage boys who said they had a gun. She coolly held her cigarette while doling out her cash, me doling out mine beside her, but after they left, she burst into tears. "That was really scary, Amy," she said. "I've never been mugged."

I had never been mugged either, but I'd been pickpocketed and groped on the train, my mom had a chain snatched off right in front of me, and my dad got jumped at the Canal Street number 1. I understood that crime was a part of New York life. But until this moment it was not a part of *hers*. I felt like a failed tour guide. Worse, I had a feeling she would stop coming to Brooklyn.

I was right. She started making excuses about the high cost of cabs, even when I said she could sleep over (I had moved to a share in Carroll Gardens for $650/month).

It had only taken her a few months to become a Manhattan snob. Even my native-Manhattanite friends were not Manhattan snobs; they were all hoping to move to Brooklyn. But New York transplants like Katherine moved to the city to become Manhattanites. She was "privileging" (to use a verb I had learned at Brown) a borough in which I never wanted to live.

Over the next few years, we began to move up in our careers. I moved to a studio apartment in Brooklyn Heights and got a regular column in the alternative weekly *New York Press* about my bad dating life. She got a job at a bigger magazine and was developing her stories in a writing class.

My column grew popular enough to get me an agent and I sold an as-yet-unwritten novel to a major publishing house for six figures. I was twenty-three. Without having planned it, I had become a writer. I quit my temping job and fired my acting agent.

I never asked Katherine if she was jealous of my deal because it would seem obnoxious and because I was a native New Yorker. Native New Yorkers don't ask their friends if they're jealous. They act humble about the good things, and they chalk their fortune up to luck instead of will.

One night, my publisher invited me to a reading and private dinner for Hunter S. Thompson to celebrate the release of *The Rum Diaries*. It was Halloween and I was Nurse Ratched—a tight, sexy nurse dress and a ratchet around my neck. Afterward we went to Pete's Tavern and I sat next to Thompson. Katherine took a photo of him with his arm around me. Benicio del Toro, who had starred in *Fear and Loathing in Las Vegas*, was at the dinner and asked us if we wanted to come to Moomba, the then-happening nightclub near Sheridan Square. We sat at a table with Thompson and del Toro, and then a group of guys came in wearing Kiss masks and someone whispered that Gene Simmons was Leonardo DiCaprio. I went over and had a very erotic conversation with Leo about my costume as I stared into the eyeholes of the mask, only to discover later that it was David Blaine.

It was a perfect New York night and we stayed out till three, and on Seventh Avenue South, in front of her cab, I waited for her to say, "Thanks for inviting me" or "That was so much fun," but she just hugged me and got inside. I chalked up what I considered her gracelessness to an inferiority complex born of the fact that she was not from New York and that her best friend, who had never planned to be a novelist, had a publishing deal.

I should explain that by this point, about three years past the day we met, our friendship had become moderately sadomasochistic. About 50 percent of the time we were together, at seemingly random intervals, she was cruel to me. If I didn't get a literary reference, she would do a little chin shake and laugh in an ugly way. If I dated a fat guy or a guy with a speech impediment and joked about it behind his back, she would mock him too heartily for my taste. Sometimes it felt like she was mocking *me*. I was like Catherine Keener dating Kevin Corrigan, Anne Heche calling him Ugly Guy.

Even though our friendship was becoming undeniably dysfunctional, I was afraid to bring it up with her. She was my best friend. I told myself she was depressed and that was why she was mean. I told myself I couldn't take it personally. Sometimes I had a boyfriend and was focused on that, and her snideness would roll right off me. Other times she had a boyfriend and was in a good mood, and when we got together, it was respectful and kind.

Soon she got a new job and a raise and her new boss was rich. She would go out with him to luxury restaurants like Woo Lae Oak on Mercer, and rarely invited me along. I had a new boyfriend by this time, a bartender and low-budget film director who wore light-colored jeans, drank tall boys, and liked to watch football. Katherine would say, "He's so different from you." I began to feel like he wasn't successful enough for her taste and it bothered me.

In the summer of 1999, I introduced Katherine to a male friend of mine, an older divorced man named Joel. Joel and I had always had a flirtatious relationship but he was in an on-and-off thing with a divorced mom and I was still with the Bud-loving filmmaker. Because I considered Joel and Katherine my closest friends, I decided they should meet. I was a native New Yorker and native New Yorkers connect people. We all sat at the bar of a Middle Eastern restaurant on Greenwich Street and then we went to her rich boss's loft, where she was crashing while he traveled. We played pool on his regulation table. I saw the way that Katherine and Joel looked at each other and wasn't surprised when she called a few days later to say they had been together every moment since I left and were now holed up in a hotel in Asbury Park.

I suspected it would end poorly but I told her I was happy. The relationship fizzled out a few weeks later and she cried all the time.

Soon after that, she met a new guy, a conceptual artist named Ken. They got serious quickly. She stopped confiding in me about her love life. The filmmaker and I broke up because I realized we *were* too different, and I dated guys so demeaning and ugly that I hid them from Katherine. By August 2001, she and I were seeing each other only once or twice a month.

I had moved into a tiny apartment in Boerum Hill overlooking the tennis bubble of New York Sports Club and behind that, the Atlantic Avenue Detention Center. She had moved in with Ken.

I went to a monastery for a *Talk* magazine article, and when I came back, after not speaking for a week, I called up Joel and we began dating. I was madly in love. We talked often about when I would tell Katherine and how she might react. I waited a month.

She and I had gone to see the Swedish film *Together* at the Angelika, and I confessed at Le Gamin on MacDougal. When I said, "Joel and I have been seeing each other," the shape of her face changed and she drank an entire glass of water. When we said goodbye, I knew something between us had died.

One morning that September, I was awakened by a call from Joel saying that a plane had flown into one of the Trade Center towers. "It must have been an accident," I said.

"I don't think it was an accident," he said.

I was lucky to be in love at that time because I had someone to talk to, and I felt safe around him, and I wasn't lonely. But downtown Brooklyn smelled like death and I would see papers blowing down the sidewalk and people walked down the street with stunned, shell-shocked faces.

By late October, I was sick of being terrified and I decided to throw a Halloween party at Roxy, a bar at Bergen and Smith where I had become a regular. I sent email invitations and when Katherine finally called, she said, "Ken is having a really hard time about the at-tacks, and he's depressed and throwing up all the time, so we're not going to be able to come."

"That's okay," I said. The line was quiet and then I said, "I'm not going to see you again, am I?"

"I've been wanting to talk to you," she said. "I'm really, really happy for you about your relationship with Joel, but I just don't feel comfort-able around you anymore and I think we need a break from each other. You always said I was your best friend, but I never felt that way about you."

I was crying big loping tears, holding the phone away to gulp air. "But why does it have to be all or nothing?" I choked out. "Why can't we hang out once in a while?"

"A friendship is kind of like a romance," she said. "At a certain point it's better to break things off completely."

Throughout the meanness and deliberate drifting and the awk-wardness of the overlapping lover, it had never occurred to me that she might someday cut me off. I believed her loyalty to me, for being her first new New York City friend, would trump everything bad be-tween us. No matter how troubled our friendship had become, she wouldn't turn her back on the person who had given her New York.

But of course, it had been coming for months, if not years. Our conversations had grown stilted because we couldn't talk about sex.

Instead we discussed minutiae, like bikini waxes, mutual friends, and whether we checked ATM receipts against bank statements. We were slowly becoming strangers.

A few weeks before the breakup, I got an email that the Actors Fund was offering tickets to Broadway plays, cheap, to help the post–September 11th economy. Somehow I got the idea that she and I should see *Rent*, even though it had already been running for five years and none of the cast members were original. Neither of us had seen it, off-Broadway or on.

We sat up high in a half-empty theater, most of the audience teenage "Rentheads" from Long Island and New Jersey who had already seen the show a dozen times. The music was tinny and miked, and there was something hollow about this ode to downtown Bohemia, when downtown was now an open grave. She sat there looking similarly miserable and I felt like she was blaming me for the play being bad.

After the show I had been invited to a birthday party at a bar in Tribeca, and she said she would come. The bar was on a side street off West Broadway. We got out at Franklin, and without the towers to indicate which way was south, I lost my sense of direction. "I think Reade Street is this way," I said, pointing.

"It's definitely not," she said. "It's this way."

"I've lived here my whole life and I know where Reade Street is." We walked two blocks before I realized, my cheeks growing hot, that she had been right. "We have to turn around," I said. "I'm sorry."

"Do you know how to get there or don't you?" she asked sullenly.

"I thought I did," I said, "but I was wrong." When we got to the bar, I held the door and she breezed past me inside.

HOT TIME IN THE OLD TOWN

Owen King

In the winter of 2004 I attended a matinee showing of *The Aviator* at the Pavilion movie theater in Park Slope, Brooklyn, with my friend Scott. I think it was January, but I know it was freezing, because I remember unraveling and unzipping and yanking off my various pieces of winter gear, and Scott piling up a big mound of our stuff in a neighboring seat. My sense of the movie, from this distant vantage, is fragmented: DiCaprio as Howard Hughes, having rules about how he wants the chocolate chips in his cookies arranged, becoming progressively crazier, crouching behind a door to talk to Alec Baldwin; Ava Gardner (Kate Beckinsale) coming to his rescue at one point; a terrible, exhilarating plane crash; one or two other moments. I remember that I liked it, basically, except a distracting thing happened during the showing, and that's what sticks with me more than the film.

"Wow," Scott whispered to me, early on, "they really have the heat cranked in here."

He was right: it was incredibly hot. I felt a trickle of sweat worming through the hair at my temple.

As the movie continued, there was a hum in the scattered audience: *It's hot, it's too hot, need to turn down the goddamn heat, sauna in here*, etc. Someone definitely went out to ask what the deal was, the result of which was that nothing perceptibly changed. It felt like it was about a hundred and five. The air in that theater had consistency; inside my mouth, I could feel it melting down, like a pat of butter on my tongue. I glanced over and saw, reflected in the screen light, slicks on Scott's face. My friend didn't look like he was watching a movie; he looked like he was observing one of the nuclear tests at Alamogordo. Meanwhile, the movie kept going, and going, and going, for about three thousand hours. Kate Hepburn was part of it. Somewhere in there, she and Howard share a bottle of milk. God, nothing ever looked so good and refreshing as that bottle of milk did that afternoon while I was slow-roasting in my fifteenth-row seat at the Pavilion.

When the movie finished, we pulled ourselves upright on wobbly, dehydrated legs. We gathered our coats, sweatshirts, gloves, scarves, and hats from the mound on the seat and began to make our way down the aisle, holding our winter gear in bundles, like inmates being released from prison.

A few rows on, near the back wall of the theater, sat a lanky, raw-boned guy, shoulder-length brown hair—he looked somewhere be-tween a surfer and a member of the Ramones—and he had his arms thrown out wide across the backs of the seats to each side of him, a dazed, postorgasmic expression on his face. He was also half-naked. His T-shirt was draped over a seat in front of him. To the waist, he was whitely bare and visibly caked in sweat.

And that's what being a New Yorker means to me: you will sooner strip naked in a movie theater than be driven from a matinee of a Scorsese movie.

I don't live in New York City anymore. I wasn't good at it. Eight years, four different apartments in Manhattan and Brooklyn, and I could still get as completely turned around on the subway as the goofiest Dubuque tourist. The cultural and recreational opportunities that only New York City offers—the clubs, the plays, the readings, the restaurants, the museums, the sporting events—generally overwhelmed me. For every concert I attended, there were twenty others I desperately wanted to see but skipped for the sedentary comfort of my apartment couch and whatever was on HBO. I am revolted by the smell of the roasted peanut carts. The omnipresent beeping that the transit trucks make when they go in reverse is my all-time number three least-favorite sound, right after nails on a chalkboard and babies screaming on airplanes. I actually kind of like Times Square. My baseball team is the Red Sox.

I live upstate now. It's quiet. Deer sleep in my backyard, curled up like cats. Everything is easier and simpler—doctors, groceries, work. No one takes off their shirt at the movie theater here.

So do I ever miss New York City?

What do you think?

I love the place. I'm so grateful for everything it gave me, and it gave me a hell of a lot. I met my wife in New York City and fell for her over drinks at a ridiculous restaurant called Nacho Mama's. One autumn night in the Bronx I saw Pedro Martinez strike out seventeen Yankees, and for most of those nine innings my team was the home team; the stadium gave up its pinstripes and roared for him, for how beautiful he was, for the glory of him, for the way he could make the ball do anything, tail and jump and limbo under bats. The hardest I've ever laughed in my life was reading, stoned off my ass in my buddy's Upper West Side apartment, the transcript in *Harper's* of Rudy Giuliani's bitter argument with a ferret rights advocate. One night after 9/11 I volunteered at a kitchen in Tribeca that was packing food for the workers, and I remember what a beautiful mix of people—young and old and women and men—had come together to do their small part.

I won't claim that any other city in the United States or, for that matter, the world would have reacted much differently to what happened in 2001. What I will state is that a lot of Americans, some of them in Congress even, detest New York City and, in fact, regard it as the least American place in America. They don't like the gays, or all the different colors of New Yorkers' skins, or all the different languages being spoken, or the atheists, or the women in the office towers who make the decisions just like the boys and screw whomever they want like the boys and spend their money on what they want like the boys. You know what I think about that point of view? I think, Sorry you feel that way. There's a box of lotioned tissues over there if you need one.

Look, you know that New York City is tough—and I'm sure that any number of people with fewer advantages than this affluent white male could tell you just how tough it can be—but at the heart of it is an idea that's as American as it gets: *If you can put up with this fucking town, then whatever else you are, you're one of us.* I treasure that bond. It's frank and it's decent and it speaks to the real bottom line, which is that our lives are so short, there's no time for bullshit.

Howard Hughes, you want a chocolate chip cookie? Great, but you'll get it the way you get it. You want to see that Scorsese movie? Super, but don't expect any special treatment. Everybody's got to share this place. We have to get along, we have to be reasonable, we have to overlook certain things, and we have to help our neighbors even if they're different, because they're our neighbors, and this town is brick and cement and the trains can never, ever stop.

CONVERSIONS: COMING OF IDENTITY IN LATE-NINETIES NEW YORK

Porochista Khakpour

Out of the more than half a million Iranians in Los Angeles—the most substantial chunk of the four million Iranians of the Iranian Diaspora—our family of four comprised half the Iranian population of South Pasadena, California, when I was growing up. There was one other Iranian family, but I was the only Iranian in not only my grade but the elementary school, middle school, and high school, at the times I was there (the other family's kids were far younger than my brother or I). Westwood's notorious "Tehrangeles," where the overwhelming majority of California's Iranians, rich and proud, set up their sparkling shops, was forty-five minutes and a whole world away. There were only two or three other kids in the school accounting for Middle Easterners in general—the popular well-dressed Egyptian sisters, one older and one younger than me; that wild Lebanese girl who claimed to be a model; and the Syrian cross-country bro with the lisp. I never exchanged more than an "excuse me" with any of them in the halls, and as far as I could tell, I was invisible to them.

My dad tried to make up for this by claiming they were all Iranian, but self hating ones who were too ashamed to bond with me.

My father's explanation for the mass migration of Iranians to Los

Angeles is one I still use today: *the climates of Tehran and Los Angeles are identical.* I also imagined seventies Iran to be a place of palm trees and glittering gold and made-up ladies draped in jewels and trendy clothes, and so I never questioned the portmanteau Tehrangeles's logic. I just knew *those* Iranians—most Iranians—who flocked to West-wood, Beverly Hills, Brentwood, and Santa Monica would certainly not have accepted us and our city, just a half hour away, a little town of twenty-five thousand, South Pasadena, a town that Hollywood would routinely film for its scarcity of staple Southern California stucco and palm trees, as the town could easily double for Midwestern and Northeastern towns. A town of NASA Jet Propulsion Lab and Caltech eccentrics, Rose Parades and Victorian homes and the first Trader Joe's was just not the stuff Iranians were made of.

As a result I could never find my footing anywhere in Los Angeles.

I dreamed of giving up crazy, conflicted California and getting as far away as possible. New York City always had the shimmer of an unofficial American capital, a place where I saw every type of human on earth converging—and not just all sorts, but the chosen ones of the all sorts. The song said if you could make it there, you could make it anywhere, and I believed it.

I started researching, picking out obvious Ivies. But then a school I had never even heard of chose me, by sending out a pamphlet that sold me simply with the motto "You Are Different. So Are We."

Their obvious clairvoyance made it the place to go. Plus they had a stellar creative writing program. Writing had always been my scholastically unexplored first love; never in school did we have even a unit in English class that took on our own poetry and prose. I had never met a creative writer in my life. And my early Internet chat-room dabblings (O AOL! O Prodigy! O dial-up!) bridged my interest in Beat culture with the still-thriving state of the East Village in the nineties. Sarah Lawrence seemed a place of writers and artists, renegades and mavericks, lesbians and vegans, rockers and rappers, a place where I could pile on identities as if they were pizza toppings, cheap and fast and easily picked off, but hopefully so amply loaded that who I actually was could be, for once, truly obscured.

They charged so much for tuition—at that point it was ranked the most expensive college in America—that they could afford to cover mine. This is what sold my parents, who wanted me to go to a University of California school. I waved my Hearst Scholarship at them, a near full ride that only required I write the trustee a long letter of my progress and gratitude each year. The assistant to the assistant dean of studies made sure I always remembered.

Sarah Lawrence College, Bronxville, New York. A twenty-five minute Metro-North ride from the city, that home I'd decided was home long before I ever set foot in it. But the college felt worlds away. Having come from suburban greater Los Angeles, suburban greater NYC felt like a bit of an insult to me. For example, one thing I did not expect was for there to be more white people than in my hometown. Here I was the only Iranian not just in my grade or school, but on the whole college campus of twelve hundred. There were again only a couple of other Middle Easterners—New York's Iranian-American population being mostly limited to the Jewish Great Neck enclave of a mere and yet relatively impressive two thousand (20 percent of Great Neck's population)—and here they were royalty, or at least acted like it. But then again everybody was somebody there; even my most normal-seeming hallmate was Peter Gabriel's daughter. While my name didn't quite stand out among the Eurydices and Harmonys and the Afrikas, at Sarah Lawrence I actually passed less than ever at first. But not because of my complexion or my hair, but because of my *clothes*. On the first day I wore jean cutoffs and Pumas and a wifebeater with no makeup and a ponytail—my Angeleno suburban trash standbys, I suppose—a lesson I learned never to repeat as I became a regular East Village shopper, blowing sometimes the whole of my parents' hundred or so sent to me every other month—just a little something to supplement my scholarship money and the Student Affairs office job I worked part-time—on something ostentatious and mostly useless, like the pair of clownish platform shoes that were the norm on Bates Hill, the "SLC runway" among the ample foliage and Tudor cottages of the campus center. My hallmates wore Prada and Gucci and gave me their high school hand-me-downs and more than once after a few drinks—amaretto, Chartreuse, Midori?—reminded me, in the wry double-bind delivery of true socialites, that their parents were paying for me to go there. They were curious about where I was from, charmed almost to know me, but often just as I'd get started with my story, they'd cut right in and move right on.

Meanwhile, the more academia stuffed me with Derrida and Chomsky, Kierkegaard and Nietzsche, Foucault and Sartre, the more difficult I found it to talk to my family. They'd rotate the phone and I'd numbly go through the motions, praying I wouldn't explode.

"What are you learning?" my mother asked.

My mother was an accountant.

"I can't get into it. Really complicated stuff. I like it."

"Are you getting good grades?"

"We don't have grades, Mom," I reminded her with a groan.

She paused. "How have you done on your tests?"

"We don't have tests here, Mom," I snapped, starting to get nasty. I would go through this weekly, it seemed.

"I'll put your dad on."

He'd get on and start grilling me about the weather for a while and then also get to the irritating stuff. "So what's your major and minor?"

"We don't have those, Dad. Do you mean my concentration?"

"What?"

"Writing," I'd say, giving up. "Just don't worry about it."

"What math are you taking?" he asked.

"I'm not."

He, a math professor, would go silent. My brother, thirteen, would get on.

"Have you gone to the Empire State? The Statue of Liberty?"

"I live in Bronxville."

"The Bronx?"

"No, never mind," I'd grumble.

"Mom says there are drugs there. Are there drugs?"

"No," I lied. "I wouldn't know."

"Do you have friends?" he asked. I could tell my mother had planted questions in him.

"Yes. Do you, nerd?"

"What are they like?"

I didn't know who was my friend and who wasn't. Even with multiple makeovers—gothish, punk-rock-lite, nerdcore-esque, hip-hippie—I never could manage to sink into a "scene." My solution to this unease was, just like in high school, to get away.

In all my undergraduate years, it was not the libraries that offered me a home, not the bookstores, not the readings, not dorms of friends and lovers, not office hours with idols, not the cubicles of internships at the greatest publications on earth, not anything but . . . the New York City nightclubs.

I spent all my time—sometimes spare, sometimes not—in clubs. Electronic music and its physical incarnation, the rave, felt like a sort of great equalizer. In the subterranean universe of gut-stabbing beats, its conversationless sea of bobbing bodies in impossibly XXXXL attire, you couldn't tell anyone apart—boy or girl, much less the mis-guided identifiers of otherness. I'd enter the arenas, clubs, and often just patches of woods, like a ghost in a dream, mind coated in the glitter of illegal psychoactive stimulants, and I'd exit straight to a deep viscous sleep, with no clear recollection of anything or anyone in that other world of mine. In a time of *self self self,* I wonder if we kept it that way—anonymous, impersonal, cool, blank—on purpose. My uniform was hoodie, cargo pants, silver chain, colorful limited-edition Nikes preferably from Japan. I could have been a boy from the warehouse next door. It was irrelevant, and yet it was intentional.

But *why*? Who was I? Why? I was, in a way, taking small steps toward self-definition, ones that had nothing to do with the body I was born in, the DNA of my parents, the blood of my ancestors. I was, for instance, a smoker, something I had taken up my freshman year in New York City. I was a yoga student. I was an occasional drug dabbler—cocaine here and there, though that was more a Sarah Lawrence sort of poison, and Ecstasy primarily in the city because of the constant promise of "pure MDMA" (from the West Coast via Europe or some other likely tall tale). I was left politically, I guessed. I was a lover of literature. Lesbian or bisexual—I constantly went back and forth about these, mainly because of my already-established love of all things alternative. I was, in the end, neither.

I was a writer, I ventured, but somehow every vision I had of that—desk, chair, pen, typewriter, books, window, dog at feet—implied that making a home was involved.

I made it through one year, then another, then I went abroad to Oxford where I spent the entire time in clubs again, clubs that reminded me of New York City.

The summer before returning to New York, the summer before my senior year, was the summer I spent in *it*—a true funk and its counterpart setting: Los Angeles. With my hood up, shielded from my native city's famed sunshine, even though it was mostly endured in my little room, with the shades drawn, among books and articles, with the phone unplugged and the door locked, I had it bad.

Electronic music meant less than anything now. Whereas the summer before I had spent giddily dating an ex–MTV VJ turned jungle DJ (in between working at the once-upon-a-time epicenter of youth cool, Urban Outfitters), now music without human presence seemed worthless, cheesy, and sometimes chilling. I turned to electronic's logical next of kin, hip-hop, all words, with some beat. But that summer the words, I remember, were angry and fearful, full of warnings and paranoias.

Pop culture was reeling from the failure of Woodstock '99, an event that had more to do with rape, looting, and arson than music. More mainstream media were in shock still over JFK Jr. and Carolyn Bessette's tragic plane crash. World news meanwhile reported that India and Pakistan were at each other's throats. And everyone was talking about the impending new year and the Y2K problem. Even 9/9/99 was causing hysteria: the computers could lose their minds, as the date value was frequently used to demarcate an unknown date, not to mention that 9999 was also an end-of-file code in old programming languages. The very near future looked ominous, and what was worse, unknowable. So loaded, it had ended up a bit blank to all of us, and that was terrifying. There were suddenly no answers.

I hid and I hid and I hid.

My father knocked on the door, and I wouldn't answer. My mother knocked on the door, and I wouldn't answer. My brother slipped me notes under the door: *It's Mom's birthday.* Or, *Can I borrow your boom box?* Once it was just, *Snap out of it, jerkass.* I knew they missed me.

I missed me.

What was my problem? Everyone wanted to know. What was my problem?

I never discovered it back then.

But today I think my real problem was I had felt on the verge of discovering a me out there in the city but I had failed somehow. All I had was a year left, senior year, to find myself, somewhere in that city, whoever I was.

There was the old familiar relief of summer's end as I boarded that flight—*phew, no more family till Christmas*—and after all those hours, the city's brashly visible landmarks had a certain nostalgia for me as we touched down. I took the bus from JFK to the city, where I arranged a ride up to Sarah Lawrence with my friend Natalya, a Ukrainian-born, Lower East Side–raised lesbian activist who was the closest thing I had to a *real* friend as well as something of an older sister to me there. She too was an outsider there, on scholarship as well, and loaded with so many minority markers she just laughed it—and everything, really—off. I met her in her family's new digs on the Upper East Side, all part of Giuliani's bizarrely idealistic plan to integrate the new poor with the very old rich.

"We live in a good time," Natalya's mom told me in her broken English as she gave me a tour of the many rooms of her high-ceiling, hardwood-floored apartment, which looked almost bare in spite of bearing all that motley stuff that had packed their LES project to near unlivability.

I nodded, numbly. They were exactly the opposite of my family: the lower class (*freakin' peasantry*, as Natalya would call them) thrust into the upper-classdom. It had given them a sort of sanity and calm. I thought of my own family: old Iranian aristocrats stuffed into a tiny, crummy suburban apartment, with nothing to show of their pedigree but the insanity of those who once had everything and were forced to abandon it all, almost overnight.

Natalya and I got to the college mostly in silence, mine largely overruling hers in a way that made her give up conversation instantly and eye me nervously the whole ride instead. On the Metro-North train, I watched Midtown become Harlem become the Bronx become finally Westchester, and I paid for our short cab ride to campus. My new dorm room was tiny and on the first floor, so I could watch everyone come and go very much on my level. And there they were: the hippies, the punk rockers, the hip-hoppers, the ravers, the goths, the mods, the butches, the femmes, the freaks. Not much had changed.

Although I had changed. I didn't realize that yet.

And so in the next month, as 9/9/99 came and went with no disturbances, I carried on, arguing with typical SLC fervor in my postmodern lit class, charging cartons of cigarettes to my parent's bookstore account, shuttling back and forth to the city for my hip *Spin* magazine internship. I carried on and on. Soon all my electronic CDs and vinyl were handed out to the late-adopter raver wannabes on my floor, and I revived my old hip-hop collection and began adding to it. Gang Starr and Tupac and old NWA began blasting out of my dorm. Not an eyebrow raised my way.

I got braided extensions to my ass, wore hoop earrings, a new sort of baggy pants, and too much makeup. I told my boss at *Spin* in a horrific fake hip-hop twang that I wanted to work at their sister magazine *Vibe*. I went to Zulu Nation meetings and asked too many questions and then straight to clubs that played hip-hop. At one point a black DJ I was hanging out with tugged at my braids and asked me if I was biracial—*half-black,* he even clarified—and I said, with little hesitation, *yes.* And then I went home and cried all night—Why had I collapsed into such a meaningless lie?—and never returned his phone calls.

This final expression of my cultural confusion was perhaps the perfect explosion—all that numbness and unknowing now grabbing at whatever it could latch onto. The lack of definition led to spontaneous definition, a stray, irresponsible, chaotic, hurtful lie. A shoplifted attempt at honest ownership. It would take the aughties to teach me, just a typical bicoastal, bicultural *other*, those real lessons.

The first lesson: I could be myself, and that self, honestly, truly, terribly did exist.

And it didn't take *all* the aughties. Just two years after that SLC homecoming, long after we all survived Y2K just fine—just past settling into my first apartment, a ramshackle Park Slope garden apartment with clashing roommates, and once I'd transitioned to my boyfriend's glossy studio, twenty-five floors up, in a then-rare East Village highrise, with a view of the entirety of Lower Manhattan and beyond—the first tear would come in the fabric, leaving you to only hope you wouldn't live long enough to see more. I woke up fast, first thing on a bright, sunny Tuesday morning, twenty-three and still in limbo—in spite of a million internships and jobs here and there, and interviews galore, I was unemployed hopelessly and had been for almost a year then—but I woke up, saw it all, and never turned back. It took nothing less than a world crumbling around me to show me who I was.

I was a New Yorker.

BROOKLYN AND ME

Adelle Waldman

For almost a decade, I rejected the idea of moving to Brooklyn. First, because Brooklyn seemed too far from the center of things and, I thought, offered primarily the sort of amenity that you might as well go to the suburbs for: more space for less money. If I was going to move to New York, I wanted to, you know, *live in New York*. Later I resisted it for a different reason. Brooklyn, far from seeming like the outskirts of town, had become too trendy. I liked to think of myself as independent-minded. I disdained "hipsters" (and was more intimidated than I wanted to admit by women who seemed impossibly cool, in a vintage clothes–wearing, bespectacled way that I admired without being able to emulate).

And so I spent ten years doing New York all wrong, ten years in which I was very often lonely and constantly on the verge of leaving.

Sure, there was an early period of infatuation when I first moved to the East Village in my early twenties. It was the late 1990s, and I felt a great sense of romance about the city and especially the neighborhood. I was happy to have found a cramped fifth-floor walk-up on East Eleventh Street—and proud I hadn't been persuaded by real estate agents to take one of those spacious one-bedrooms in some distant

Brooklyn neighborhood called Park Slope. I did love Alphabet City back then—the used bookstores, the dive bars, the dog run at Tompkins Square Park. I especially loved the cafés and coffee shops—the grungy ones you could still smoke in, full of bike messengers reading Nietzsche or grad school dropouts turned bartenders, i.e., people wholly different from the types I knew from college, whose concerns revolved around grades and GPAs and law school. It didn't matter that I barely knew anyone in the city. The streets themselves felt like a party, the kind of party I most wanted to be invited to, full of passionate, interesting nonconformists.

Although I didn't know enough to appreciate this quality back then—I recognized it only years later, long after it was gone—I was open to new experiences in a way I think is characteristic of youth, a way that is both admirable for its adventurousness but also a bit tainted by the narcissistic desire to live life as if it were for a story you were telling someone later. Back then, if I was bored, I might sit at a coffee shop and read and people-watch, and end up in a long conversation about the neighborhood's history with a silver-haired man whose grandchildren were around my age. I might walk to Washington Square Park to play chess for a few bucks a game. I had long conversations with strangers—and not merely potential dates, in my "demographic." I remember a set designer in his early fifties and clearly gay. He approached me when he saw I was reading George Eliot in Tompkins Square Park. I never saw him again, and yet I've never forgotten him. He said his favorite Eliot novel was *Romola*, an unusual choice. Years later, when I used a line from *Romola* as my novel's epigraph, I thought of him. I also became friendly with the guys who worked at the parking lot next door to my apartment building and who hung out on the sidewalk when there were no cars to park. When I baked, I brought them brownies and cookies. After I dropped a bottle of wine so that it shattered outside my building's front door—I was coming home with supplies for a dinner party—one of my parking lot friends gave me a present of a box of wine, which, he noted drily, I was unlikely to break.

I loved New York that first year. I wasn't lonely. But something happened. Nothing and everything. The banalities of adult life overtook the city's romance. I left the East Village for Queens to move in with a boyfriend. It didn't work out. I moved back to Manhattan, to a worse apartment than the one I'd left. I went from waitressing to a professional job, working as a reporter for a financial trade publication. The company was called Institutional Investor. I got a subscription to the *Wall Street Journal* and often worked late. I didn't bake as much, and I didn't spend time chatting with guys who hung out on the sidewalk. I became very concerned with paying back the credit card debt I'd racked up in that first irresponsible year and a half of waitressing and frequent relocations. I entered into a new relationship, which, unlike the one that had taken me to Queens, would last for a number of years and which felt very grown-up in ways that were both good and bad. By my midtwenties, New York no longer felt like a constant party. It was just the place where I lived. As time went on, that meant it would be the backdrop for a lot of unhappiness.

One of the biggest sources of unhappiness was my dissatisfaction as a writer. I worked as a financial reporter, but I wanted to be a novelist. However, I had yet to write a word of decent fiction, which caused me some anxiety but did nothing to improve the quality of my writing. When I was twenty-six, I went to journalism school, believing that journalism was a good day job for an aspiring novelist and that journalism school would lead to a more interesting reporting job than the one at Institutional Investor or the one I'd had after that, at a small newspaper in Connecticut. I thought—correctly—that grad school would help me to get a job at a better newspaper. I went to Columbia, which brought me to Morningside Heights, a neighborhood that didn't have the same romance for me as the East Village. It was also far from most of my friends, who increasingly lived in Brooklyn. But I had a good deal on a rent-stabilized apartment.

After journalism school, I got an internship at the *Plain Dealer*, a newspaper in Cleveland, and because it was just an internship, I held on to the rent-stabilized apartment, subletting it to two friends from school. When my internship was extended, my subletters stayed on. When, after about eight months, the *Plain Dealer* offered me a full-time job, I didn't know what to do. By then the long-term boyfriend and I had broken up, our pseudo grown-up relationship having devolved into a rather strained and joyless version of adult life. Even though my life in Manhattan hadn't thrilled me in years, being newly single in Cleveland wasn't great either. In the end, I declined the job. I decided to return to New York to make a go at being a freelance writer. After all, I had an affordable apartment waiting for me. How many people could say that?

Things didn't go quite as I hoped. Freelancing was harder than I expected, both financially and, more surprisingly, emotionally. I considered myself an independent, readerly type of person. I liked solitude, or so I believed. Then I discovered that being alone for the whole workday made feel a little sad and a little crazy—a realization that poked a little hole in my proud self-conception. My previous jobs, from Institutional Investor through the *Plain Dealer*, had provided with me more, psychologically, than I had realized, had been more than paychecks and experience for the résumé. At home by myself, I became the kind of person who constantly emailed friends about nothing. "How is your morning?" I'd write to Alexis at eleven a.m. "What did you do last night?" I'd write half an hour later, forgetting that Alexis didn't need to spend her day shooting the shit with me. She had real live coworkers to do that with.

I began dating a reporter for a New York paper and felt an acute power imbalance unlike anything I'd have anticipated. My boyfriend's days were spent with coworkers or in packs of photographers and reporters from competing papers as they waited for hours at a time outside a subject's home or office. At the end of the day, he simply wasn't as hungry for companionship as I was. Plus he was often drawn into spontaneous happy-hour drinks after work, the way I had once been—back when I had coworkers. Because of his job, he was regularly invited to all sorts of fancy parties. It didn't matter that most of the parties weren't especially appealing—they were PR events for new products or companies—it was the principle. No one invited me to their PR events, not now that I was just a freelancer.

Most important, I didn't much like the work I was doing. I mostly wrote business stories for newspapers and trade publications, but I hoped to do more arts and culture writing and to break into magazines. For the first year or so that I worked freelance, I imagined happiness was just one promising assignment away—all I needed was for some magazine editor to give me a shot—but I found myself losing heart as time went on and no one did (somehow I had thought good things would just happen if I lived in New York and was freelance—i.e., threw myself in fate's path). Besides, I was so focused on trying to get enough work to pay the rent that I didn't have that much energy left to strategize about orchestrating my big break. Soon I lost any belief that I was moving forward, toward something better.

Why, you might be wondering, if I was so unhappy, didn't I pack it up and get a regular job? All I can say is I think something happens to people who've freelanced for a while. At least it happened to me. Even if you begin by choice, after a time you start to feel unemployable—somehow inferior, marked out for a strange and marginal existence, distinct from that of those well-socialized full-timers whose company-sponsored email addresses and holiday parties are, like engagement rings, proofs that they are loved—or at least claimed. That's how I felt, anyway. I assume it's different for people who freelance at a higher level than I did, who win National Magazine Awards and get flown across the world to conduct interviews with world leaders.

By my late twenties, I was—I won't say unhappy in my career, because "career" seems too lofty and grandiose a term for what I was doing then: writing tedious columns about personal finance for low pay and no benefits. Let's just say I was unhappy professionally. My personal life was also a bust. The newspaper reporter and I had long since gone our separate ways, and I wondered how likely I was to meet anyone new when my work life was conducted from home and consisted mostly of telephone calls to middle-aged financial advisers who lived with their families in the suburbs. Plus, I lived so far from most of my friends—an hour subway's ride to Brooklyn—that I saw them relatively rarely, when we made plans to meet up for a meal in downtown Manhattan, often at some too-loud restaurant.

The unhappier I got, the more isolated I became. I had less and less desire to get together with a certain type of casual friend, the kind for whom you feel compelled to put on at least a moderately good face, to present your life in terms that are not entirely depressing. Some friends energize and others enervate, a good friend of mine (an energizer) once noted—and when you feel the way I did, a much higher percentage enervate.

My unhappiness made me ashamed. I had become a lonely, professionally stalled single woman in a city that is said to be full of such women, and a culture that is often contemptuous of us, that makes jokes about cat ladies, that both pities and blames us. (I'm not sure which is worse.) That my unhappiness was so commonplace, so clichéd made it all the worse. I had once, with the arrogance of youth, thought I'd never be that kind of woman; I was too ambitious, too passionate in my intellectual interests, too willing to work hard to ever become someone who would be categorized this way, whether or not

I was romantically attached. My belief that I was different from other women was the kind of personal exceptionalism that ought to get shucked off as one grows older, and yet the process of ridding oneself of comforting illusions is, of course, painful.

The most important thing I did—perhaps the only important thing—during those years was read. I read not just obsessively but in a disciplined, programmatic way, going through the entire body of one author after another. Since my early twenties, I'd been drawn to eighteenth- and nineteenth-century writers. This taste for older books was invaluable for me as a writer, but it had drawbacks for me as a social human being. I wasn't getting excited about new fiction and going to readings where it's possible I might have met actual flesh-and-blood people whom I could become friends with. I worked alone, and at night I read alone, often with a bottle of red wine in lieu of company. I assumed—rather myopically, it turns out—that this was pretty much what everybody did. I thought New York was a sad city, a place full of trapped, isolated people hungering for connection.

I was so desperate that, at twenty-nine, I returned to my old bedroom in my parents' house in suburban Baltimore. It was just going to be for six months; my plan was to write a novel in that time and then return to New York. Now or never, I told myself. I quit the personal finance column and sublet my apartment. Still, no one was more surprised than I was when I actually pulled it off. I produced a 550-page document that could only be called a novel, with a large cast of characters and a plot consisting of a beginning, a middle, and an end.

I returned to New York with the taste of triumph in my mouth. I thought I'd send the novel to literary agents and soon have a publishing deal. I wasn't eager to return to my lackluster freelance lifestyle, so instead I found work as an SAT tutor. I figured I'd only be doing it for a few months, until my book sold and I was too busy being interviewed by the likes of Terry Gross. I was an SAT tutor for seven years.

The year I turned thirty felt like a very long one. Over the course of many months, I came to realize that no one wanted to publish that novel. Rejection is always hard. This one seemed like not only a reflection on my writing; in practical terms, it felt like my last hope had been extinguished.

But one important piece of luck had befallen me that year. An old friend from high school had come to New York to do a postdoc at Columbia. He moved into my spare room. If he hadn't been there that year—cheering me up, distracting me with talk of *his* life and *his* problems, or initiating long conversations about life and art and politics—I'm not really sure how I would have gotten through. What a different place New York was when you interacted regularly with other humans. When Matt moved out in the spring, I decided to give up the Morningside Heights apartment, no matter how good a deal I had. I didn't want to be lonely again. I had to make a change. I wanted to be around people I related to; I had to move to Brooklyn. The desire to see myself as different—as not the kind of writer who would live in Brooklyn like all the others—was a luxury I could no longer afford.

Objectively, moving to Brooklyn seemed like a fairly desperate move. After all, they say that moving doesn't change anything because you bring yourself—and by extension your problems—with you. Well, I am here to tell you that this is not always the case.

What I had previously thought of as life in New York—cold, solitary, gray—turned out to have been merely *my* life in New York. When I moved nearer to the few friends I was still fairly close to, I met their other friends, the ones they saw all the time because they bumped into each other in the neighborhood and grabbed impromptu cups of coffee. I didn't know that people in New York sometimes called each other up and suggested meeting up *that very afternoon or evening*, in an hour or two. I had assumed that kind of casual socializing had gone the way of 1950s-style double dates to the movies and soda shop. It turns out that not living an hour's train ride from your friends helps. (Who knew?) I became closer to my old friends, whom I not only saw more of but saw in ways that were more meaningful—not just at restaurants but for walks in the park or at our apartments for home-cooked meals and drinks and late-night talks. I also, seemingly effortlessly, made new friends.

None of this solved my overarching life problems—it didn't make my unpublished novel get published or make SAT tutoring any more satisfying—but it made me a great deal happier, happier than I had thought possible after the years of slowly accruing loneliness. It's easy to mock Brooklyn for its superabundance of writers and publishing types, the stupefying number of people walking around carrying tote bags from one or another independent bookstore or book publisher. But I have come to believe that there are far worse things than a place full of people who like to read.

About a year after I moved to Brooklyn, a guy I'd begun dating (a friend of a friend) encouraged me to begin another novel. He thought the time had come for me to quit moaning about the one that didn't get published: it was time to move forward. He was right. The experience of writing that first novel had taught me two very important things: that I could write a novel—which was more than I knew for most of my twenties—and that I really liked doing it.

I began a new novel. Perhaps because I had felt isolated for so long, I took a rather anthropological interest in Brooklyn's literary scene and used it as the setting for this novel, dissecting it through the eyes of my protagonist, a far more successful—and less lonely—free-lancer than I'd been.

This novel took me four years to write. I wasn't buoyed by giddy exuberance the way I had been when I wrote my first one. I knew that writing a novel doesn't mean that it will be published. I was also, as the years went on, increasingly anxious about being a thirty-something tutor. When strangers asked me what I did for a living, I didn't know how to respond. Could I really say I was a writer? According to my tax returns, I was not a working writer but a tutor with a Microsoft Word document.

But I was also among friends, to a degree I hadn't been since college, and this made a tremendous difference. With my friends, many of whom were also writers, I didn't feel like a failed novelist/journalist or an overaged tutor. My friends took my novel seriously. As I wrote, I gave it to several of them chapter by chapter. Some of my fondest memories of those years are sitting in the spare, book-lined living room of my friend Melissa's apartment, with her roommate, discussing my latest chapter—or Melissa's roommate's latest—over too much wine as we occasionally huddled by an open window to smoke a cigarette (technically I'd quit years ago, but I made exceptions). The other person who read the novel chapter by chapter was my boyfriend, the one who encouraged me to begin. (He's now my husband.) Other friends read it in chunks. Their comments were helpful, but what was even more helpful was being among people who treated novel writing as my "real" job, never mind that I had no agent or publisher or guarantee of success, that I'd never published a word of fiction.

This may sound minor, but it wasn't, at least not to me. To be taken seriously as a fiction writer helped me through the difficult stretches. It offset some of the discouragement that I, like most unpublished fiction writers, got plenty of. Many people in my life knew what had happened with my first novel and were concerned about my future, worried I was wasting valuable time on a childish dream. They figured, not unreasonably, that if I'd been any good, the first novel would have been published. This was not unkind; they wanted to protect me from more disappointment.

What I appreciated most about my writer friends was not that they built me up with grand hopes but that they knew how publishing worked and knew me and were cautiously optimistic. One can feel beaten down by pessimists who tell you that "nobody" unknown or unconnected ever gets published, but the well-meaning certainty of affectionate but naïve friends—those lovely, loving people who assure you that as soon as you finish your novel, it'll be picked by Oprah, since after all you've been a great writer "since kindergarten!"—can also be problematic. Measured optimism, grounded in knowledge, is a real comfort.

Almost five years to the day after I moved to Brooklyn, *The Love Affairs of Nathaniel P.* was published. Some people read the book as a satire of Brooklyn, but to me the mockery comes from a place of deep fondness. The world of the novel, a world full of aspiring writers, is, I think, troublesome in terms of certain gender dynamics; it is also permeated with a grating status consciousness. But I don't think sexism or status consciousness are unique to Brooklyn—and I think the Brooklyn of the novel, like the real Brooklyn, offers other compensations, in terms of community.

Of course, I don't think that every writer needs to live in Brooklyn, or New York, or needs writer friends. It's personal. And an aspiring novelist who does want a community of writers can surely find it in other ways—an MFA program comes to mind. (I didn't take that path because, rightly or wrongly, I believed my literary tastes and particular novelistic ambitions were out of step with MFA values.) All I can say is that for me, community turned out to be more important than I realized when I was young—important to a degree that is humbling—and I happened to find it in Brooklyn.

The New York that is dear to me, the one that took me ten years to find—because I am slow and stubborn and prone to missteps—has nothing to do with celebrity or wealth or five-star restaurants or, for that matter, organic vegetables or artisanal anything. New York for me is a group of people who, in my early thirties, meant the world to me, a group of not-quite-struggling-but-not-quite-arrived writers who supported each other over endless cups of coffee and glasses of wine, who listened to one another's romantic travails and learned about each other's families and read and believed in one another's work.

THE REPLACEMENTS

Nick Flynn

On one of those days the radio tells us is dangerous to be alive, the air so thick it will kill you, an *air advisory* day, I biked from Brooklyn (where I lived and have always lived since landing here) over the Williamsburg Bridge to the Strand. It was my first summer in New York, I was kneeling in the poetry section because that's where I go, and when I went to get up I felt a woozy head rush. I was overheated and really felt I would collapse then and there and I knew if I did they would simply roll me out onto the sidewalk and I would become part of the detritus. If I fell I would end up like Jimi Hendrix in the back of that last ambulance in Seattle—*Just another black junkie*, the EMTs said (though I was neither black nor a junkie)—and they would drive around with me in the back, no rush, until we were all dead. That was the day I realized that as far as New York was concerned (if New York could be imagined as a living being, like a hive), I was utterly and completely and immediately replaceable. New York didn't give a fuck about me unless it was able to suck out some energy: this was in fact what kept the city spinning. To New York we are all simply energy cells, especially the young, to be sucked dry and discarded. It is brutal and mean and all the glamour is empty, just like everywhere, except here the good guys and the bad guys dress exactly alike (hipsters) so you never know who you're talking to—rapacious capitalist? Idiot savant? Junkie trickster?

Here is the moment where I am supposed to say, *And yet . . .* but I'm not ready, not yet, for that. Maybe it's because we're all frozen in that first moment we stepped foot on the island, maybe that's why the fact that it hasn't noticed us, all these years, feels so stark. My first moment was when I was about five. We drove down from Massachusetts with a boyfriend of my mother's (David? Bert?) and went to Ripley's Believe It or Not, where a man who had pulled out his own hair and eyelashes and fingernails had built a statue of himself out of them. We went to the top of the Empire State Building, my mother cautioning that I would kill someone on the sidewalk below if I threw a penny down, that it would pass clean through his entire body (this was a lie). We went to the Automat for a futuristic lunch—tuna fish sandwiches and slices of pie behind little glass doors that opened when you put coins in. But mostly what I remember was seeing a man sleeping on the sidewalk. It looked like one of his eyes was dripping out of his head. I swear I saw that.

A few years later my junior high social studies class took a bus down—a field trip—maybe forty of us. We went to the UN and to the newly opened World Trade Center and to see a magician (Doug Henning) in an afternoon show (Dustin Hoffman was in the audience and signed my program). I bought some magic cards and dropped them in the middle of Fifth Avenue and traffic had to stop and honk as I collected them all. I still have photographs from that trip, each with a white border around it. Now you can buy an app to re-create that white border "effect," if you want the photo to seem to come from the past, even though they all do anyway.

Ten years after that I drove my new pal Richard from Provincetown in my pickup truck back to his loft on Trinity Place. He'd fled a few months earlier to escape a nasty heroin habit and now we were back to pack up his stuff. We went out dancing to the Palladium and Area, places Richard had sometimes worked. My mother had died a couple of years earlier and then Area closed and then the Palladium closed and then Richard died and by the time I moved to Brooklyn it was as if everything I knew or had known was slipping through my fingers. This is mostly what I feel and mostly what I've felt since I landed here, twenty years ago now—that I wander a city of the no-longer-there.

After my near-death experience in the poetry aisles of the Strand, I was free of the illusion that New York gave a fuck whether I lived or died, whether I stayed or left. In this way New York began to correspond with my vague and ever-shifting concept of God. Whatever hole I left would be filled, whatever apartment I vacated would be rented, whatever job I fled would be filled, all in an instant. If I was missed, there were twenty poetry readings that night and twenty openings and twenty parties and twenty possible lovers that would all fill in whatever tiny void my passing left.

What did I do with this sobering knowledge? I left, of course, many, many times. I tried Europe, Mexico, Africa, Vietnam, anywhere. Seattle? I tried—wrong ocean. The sun set *into* the ocean in Seattle and that was wrong—the sun is supposed to rise from the ocean, as it always did. I tried to leave, again and again. I would disappear for a week or a year and when I came back, anyone I ran into on the street would simply look happy to see me (or avert their eyes, depending on how we'd left it) but it was as if we had spoken yesterday, not a year ago.

But there was something in this—in the fact that I would run into someone on the streets, each day, invariably, someone from a moment in my long history with the city—that began to add up to something, some *texture*. Whenever I left I found myself missing precisely this— these random encounters. Each day, any day I venture out of my apartment, which is most days I wake up in New York, it will happen. I will, if I open my eyes, run into someone, randomly, either on the sidewalk or on the subway or in a coffee shop or a bookstore, someone from one of the decades of my life. Last week I ran into Marty outside a café in the West Village; he was talking to Sam about a play they might do together. Then I ran into Elissa outside a drugstore on Sixth; her daughter is now seventeen. I saw an ex on the A train platform outside Penn Station, standing with someone I imagined was her new lover. We were all heading downtown, we hadn't seen each other in years or spoken, and we didn't that day, but we saw each other, we were still both alive.

Sometimes the seemingly random is not all that random. I go to an opening and there will be artists there I know, or I go to a reading and there will be writers. Which artist or which writer is the wild card, but there will always be at least one I will spend some time with and we make a plan to get together, but even if we don't, this is enough. I get around the city by bicycle, which makes these encounters either more or less likely, I don't know the math (I'm covering more ground but moving faster). My friend Doug, my friend Tom have both mentioned seeing me ride past and not calling out for fear I would crash. Were those random encounters, even if we didn't speak?

Last year I moved to Vancouver with my family for an indefinite period of time (it turned into seven months), and I knew even before I got there that I would never have a random encounter, not in Vancouver— since I knew no one there, it would simply be impossible—and I was right. After I'd been in Vancouver for four months (four months without a random encounter), I flew back to New York for a reading and, stepping out of the taxi a block from my apartment, I ran into Eli—Eli of Provincetown in 1999 and Rome in 2001—and it was as if we'd seen each other yesterday, as if I'd never left. It was at that moment I realized how important these encounters are to me, but I can't say why.

I'm married, I have a child, all that is very, very good, yet there was an energy of first being in New York, the possibility, no, the certainty, that anything could happen, and that whatever happened would set in motion the rest of your life. It was before my life had started, I now see. I saw a beautiful girl one morning, I was on a corner on the Lower East Side, she came up and asked, *Are you looking too?* I knew she meant heroin, and if I said yes we would go and find it, but I didn't say yes. A couple of years later I arranged to meet a blind date in a café near that corner, a place I'd write in for an hour on my way home to Brooklyn (I can't remember the name of it and now it is gone). As I walked in I saw a different woman at each table and it seemed any one of them could be my future. As it was, the blind date and I stayed together for two years, and she did change my life. I run into her sometimes; it means something that we were together. New York will keep on spinning with or without us, but this is the part that isn't replaceable.

ABOUT THE CONTRIBUTORS

One of the country's preeminent singer/songwriters, **ROSANNE CASH** has released fifteen albums of extraordinary songs that have earned her a Grammy Award and nominations for twelve more, as well as twenty-one top forty hits, including eleven number one singles. She is also an author of four books, including the bestselling memoir *Composed*, which the *Chicago Tribune* called "one of the best accounts of an American life you'll likely ever read." Her essays have appeared in the *New York Times*, *Rolling Stone*, *The Oxford American*, the Huffington Post, and many more print and online publications. In recent seasons, Cash has given concerts at the Spoleto Festival, Toronto's Luminato Festival, and New Haven's Festival of Arts and Ideas, and partnered in programming collaborations with the Minnesota Orchestra, New York's Lincoln Center, and San Francisco Jazz. She recently completed a residency at the Library of Congress.

Her recent album *The List* won the Americana Music Album of the Year award. She was given the AFTRA Lifetime Achievement Award for Sound Recordings in 2012.

In her latest release, *The River and the Thread*, a collaboration with husband/cowriter/producer/arranger John Leventhal, Cash evokes a kaleidoscopic examination of the geographic, emotional, musical, and historic landscape of the American South. The album has received impressive worldwide acclaim and attained the highest debut in the Billboard charts of any of her albums.

ALEXANDER CHEE is the author of the novels *Edinburgh* and the forthcoming *The Queen of the Night*. He is a winner of the Whiting and the NEA in fiction, and his stories and essays have appeared in *Tin House, TriQuarterly, Apology,* the Morning News, and the *New York Times Sunday Book Review*. He lives in New York City.

JASON DIAMOND is an associate editor at *Men's Journal*, the former literary editor at Flavorwire, the founder of Vol. 1 Brooklyn, and has had his work published by the *New York Times*, the *Paris Review, Tablet, New York* magazine, the *New Republic*, and many other places. He lives in Brooklyn with his wife, two cats, and a dog named Max.

STEPHEN ELLIOTT is the author of seven books, including *The Adderall Diaries*. In 2012 his directorial debut, *About Cherry*, was released by IFC. His second feature film, *Happy Baby*, will be released in 2015. He is the founding editor of the online literary site The Rumpus.

PATRICIA ENGEL is the author of *It's Not Love, It's Just Paris* (Grove 2013), and *Vida* (Grove 2010), which was a *New York Times* Notable Book of the Year and a finalist for the PEN/Hemingway and Young Lions Fiction Awards. Her fiction has appeared in the *Atlantic, A Public Space, Boston Review,* and *Harvard Review*, among others. Most recently she is the recipient of a 2014 fellowship in prose from the National Endowment for the Arts. She is at work on a novel and currently lives in Miami.

ISAAC FITZGERALD has been a firefighter, worked on a boat, and been given a sword by a king, thereby accomplishing three out of five of his childhood goals. He has also written for the Bold Italic, McSweeney's Internet Tendency, *Mother Jones*, and the *San Francisco Chronicle*. He is the co-owner of The Rumpus, co-founder of Pen & Ink, and editor of BuzzFeed Books.

NICK FLYNN is the author of *Another Bullshit Night in Suck City* and *The Captain Asks for a Show of Hands*, as well as other books. He lives in Brooklyn.

ELIZABETH GILBERT's essay "The Muse of the Coyote Ugly Saloon," first published in the March 1997 issue of *GQ* and reprinted in this collection, was the basis for the motion picture *Coyote Ugly*.

Gilbert is best known for her 2006 memoir *Eat, Pray, Love*, which chronicled her journey alone around the world, looking for solace after a difficult divorce. The book was an international bestseller, translated into over thirty languages with more than 10 million copies sold worldwide. In 2010, *Eat, Pray, Love* was made into a film starring Julia Roberts. The book became so popular that *Time* magazine named Gilbert one of the hundred most influential people in the world.

In 2010, Gilbert published *Committed*, a follow-up to *Eat, Pray, Love*, which explored her ambivalence about the institution of marriage.

Her latest novel, *The Signature of All Things*, published in autumn 2013, is a sprawling tale of nineteenth-century botanical exploration. She is also the author of the story collection *Pilgrims*, the novel *Stern Men*, and *The Last American Man*, a biography about modern woodsman Eustace Conway.

WHOOPI GOLDBERG is an actor, director, producer, recording artist, and author. In 2002, she became one of a very elite group of artists who have won a Grammy ("Whoopi Goldberg: Direct from Broadway," 1985), an Academy Award (*Ghost*, 1990), a Golden Globe (*The Color Purple*, 1985, and *Ghost*, 1990), a Daytime Emmy (co-host of "The View" in 2009, on which she continues to appear, and host of *Beyond Tara: The Extraordinary Life of Hattie McDaniel*, 2002), and a Tony (producer of *Thoroughly Modern Millie*, 2002). She is equally well known for her humanitarian efforts on behalf of children, the homeless, human rights, education, substance abuse, and the battle against

AIDS, as well as many other causes and charities, and is a Goodwill Ambassador to the United Nations.

In 1992, Whoopi made her debut as an author with her first children's book, *Alice*. Her second literary endeavor, simply titled *Book*, became a bestseller in the U.S. and around the world. Hyperion Books published *Whoopi's Big Book of Manners* in 2006 and launched the Sugar Plum Ballerinas book series for young readers in 2008 with *Plum Fantastic*, followed by *Toeshoe Trouble*, *Perfectly Prima*, *Terrible Terrel*, *Sugar Plums to the Rescue!*, and *Dancing Diva*. *Is It Just Me?* is her most recent book for adults.

JON-JON GOULIAN is the author of *The Man in the Gray Flannel Skirt*, a memoir of androgyny. His other work includes a recent essay for *Vice* called "In Defense of Hairy Women" about his fetish for female body hair. He lives in Los Angeles.

KATHLEEN HALE is the author of *No One Else Can Have You* and the forthcoming novel *Nothing Bad Is Going to Happen*. She lives in Brooklyn.

COLIN HARRISON is the editor-in-chief of Scribner and the author of seven novels, six of which are set in New York City. He has lived in Brooklyn since 1987.

ANNA HOLMES is a California-born-and-bred writer and editor living in New York.

Her work has appeared in the *New York Times*, the *Washington Post*, and the *New Yorker* online. She is the editor of two books, 2002's *Hell Hath No Fury: Women's Letters from the End of the Affair*, and 2013's *The Book of Jezebel*, which is based on the popular women's website she created in 2007. Her favorite NYC borough is Queens.

ELLIOTT KALAN is a comedian, head writer and three-time Emmy winner for *The Daily Show with Jon Stewart*, and cohost of the bad-movie podcast the Flop House. He has also written superhero stories for Marvel Comics, articles on the 1939 New York World's Fair, and the best-ever unproduced screenplay about a real estate–themed vigilante attempting to stop a secret society of ninjas from resurrecting a demonic Robert Moses. Follow him on Twitter: @elliottkalan.

POROCHISTA KHAKPOUR is the author of the novels *The Last Illusion* (May 2014, Bloomsbury) and *Sons and Other Flammable Objects* (2007, Grove), the latter of which was a 2007 California Book Award winner in first fiction, one of the *Chicago Tribune*'s "Fall's Best," and a *New York Times* editor's choice. Her writing has appeared or is forthcoming in *Harper's*, the *New York Times*, the *Los Angeles Times*, Slate, Salon, the Daily Beast, *Spin*, *Elle*, NPR, and in many other publications around the world. She is currently Writer in Residence at Bard College and Visiting Writer at Wesleyan University. Born in Tehran and raised in Los Angeles, she lives in New York City.

OWEN KING is the author of the novel *Double Feature*. His writing has appeared in *Grantland*, the *Los Angeles Review of Books*, *One Story*, and *Prairie Schooner*, among other publications. He is married to the novelist Kelly Braffet.

JULIE KLAM is the author of *Please Excuse My Daughter*, *You Had Me at Woof*, *Love at First Bark*, and *Friendkeeping*, all Riverhead Books. She writes for various publications, including the *New York Times Book Review*. She lives in Manhattan (duh).

MARIS KREIZMAN is the creator of Slaughterhouse 90210, a blog that celebrates the intersection of her two great loves—literature and

TV. *Slaughterhouse 90210: The Book* will be published by Flatiron Books in 2015. A former book editor, Maris cannot get enough of critiquing her own writing.

PHILLIP LOPATE is an essayist, novelist, and poet, and the author of more than a dozen books, including *Waterfront*, *Portrait Inside My Head*, and *To Show and to Tell: The Craft of Literary Nonfiction*. He is also the editor of the anthologies *Writing New York*, *American Movie Critics*, and *The Art of the Personal Essay*. He is a professor of writing at Columbia University, where he directs the graduate nonfiction program.

BRIAN MACALUSO is a musician, writer, and storyteller who lives in the mid–Hudson Valley. He worked for many years in New York City recording studios such as Electric Lady. He currently owns and runs Tech Smiths, the Hudson Valley's only Apple Authorized Service Provider.

SUSAN ORLEAN is the author of eight books, including *The Orchid Thief*, *Rin Tin Tin: The Life and the Legend*; and *The Bullfighter Checks Her Makeup*. She has been a staff writer for the *New Yorker* since 1992. Her subjects have included umbrella inventors, origami artists, skater Tonya Harding, gospel choirs, and backyard chickens. Her work has also appeared in *Esquire*, *Rolling Stone*, *Outside*, and the *New York Times*, and was the basis of the films *Adaptation* and *Blue Crush*.

Orlean graduated from the University of Michigan and was a Nieman Fellow at Harvard University. She has lived in Portland, Oregon; Boston, Massachusetts; New York City; and Pine Plains, New York. She now divides her time between the Hudson Valley and Studio City, California, along with her husband, son, one dog, two cats, eight chickens, and four turkeys.

AMY SOHN is the author of *The Actress, Prospect Park West,* and three other novels. She has been a columnist at *New York* magazine, the *New York Post, Grazia,* and *New York Press.* She lives in Brooklyn with her husband and daughter.

ADAM STERNBERGH is a contributing writer to *New York* magazine and the former culture editor of the *New York Times Magazine.* He's also the author of the suspense novel *Shovel Ready,* set in a near-future dystopian New York, and its sequel, *Near Enemy.* His writing has also appeared in *GQ* and the *Times* of London, and he's appeared on the radio program *This American Life.* He (still) lives in Brooklyn.

In RACHEL SYME's dreams, she is six and lives inside the Plaza Hotel. But in real life, she is a writer and historian living in an apartment with tin ceilings in Brooklyn who contributes to the *New Yorker,* NPR, the *New York Times, New York* magazine, and other publications online and off around town. She is hard at work on her first book, a biography of F. Scott Fitzgerald during his tempestuous Hollywood years, for Random House, due out fall 2015(ish). She owes most of her identity (and certainly her ability to walk miles in four-inch platforms) to New York City and thanks her lucky stars every day that her parents bought her that first plane ticket out.

ADELLE WALDMAN is the author of the novel *The Love Affairs of Nathaniel P.*

JENNA WORTHAM is a technology reporter for the *New York Times* and lives in Brooklyn.

ACKNOWLEDGMENTS

O ften I marvel at my good fortune in not just once but *twice* (so far) managing to wrangle some of my favorite authors into books I've been lucky enough to edit. Getting to do this work, with writers I hold in the highest esteem, is a fantasy come true. I can't thank all my incredible contributors enough.

Rayhane Sanders championed and agented this book without benefit of a proper proposal, leaving me awed and most grateful. She landed it in the incredibly deft hands of Lauren Spiegel at Simon & Schuster's Touchstone Books, who has been not just a smart, savvy editor but also a great wrangler herself. A big thanks to her and everyone at Touchstone and Simon & Schuster.

Thanks, once again, to Brooke Warner, Laura Mazer, Eva Zimmerman, and everyone at Seal Press for their great work on *Goodbye to All That: Writers on Loving and Leaving New York*, the first anthology, of which this is a follow-up. And thanks to all of the great women writers who contributed to that book.

James Gulliver Hancock once again provided wonderful illustrations that capture perfectly the city I love. (Incidentally, the building on the cover of *Goodbye to All That* bears a striking resemblance to the East Village tenement I lived in for nearly a dozen years and was selected independently of me without anyone else's knowledge of that. *Spooky.*)

Omega Institute's Women's Leadership Center generously granted me a weeklong residency in their nicest cabin at their beautiful retreat center in Rhinebeck. The crew at Outdated Café in Kingston, New York, kept me in gluten-free treats and rocket fuel–grade coffee as I hung out and worked for hours on end. And the crew at 3B B&B in downtown Brooklyn made it affordable for me to come down from upstate and stay over for appointments and events. They also made me scrumptious breakfasts that were gluten-free (and adhered to my other peculiar dietary preferences without judgment).

Thanks, too, to the city friends who have let me stay with them, or loaned me their apartments when they've been away, allowing me to pretend, briefly, that I live there again: Ann Klein and Tim Hatfield; Huck Hirsch and Jim Brodsky; Kevin and Emily Mandel; Emily Gould and Keith Gessen; and Jennifer Nix and Steve Leonard.

Thanks to Stephen Elliott, Isaac Fitzgerald, and everyone at The Rumpus for so many connections, and for your patience with how long I've gone between installments of my column as I've juggled this and other high-pressure commitments.

Eva Tenuto, my friend and executive director of TMI Project (TMIProject.org), was supportive in many ways, including providing gainful employment and letting me take some time off to finish editing this.

My family has cheered me on (and sometimes lent a hand, financially); I will be forever grateful.

Last but not least, my husband, Brian Macaluso, has not only been my greatest support, this time he's also contributed his own essay to the collection. How's that for a happy ending?

232 // NEVER CAN SAY GOODBYE

About the Editor

SARI BOTTON is a writer living in Kingston, New York, whose work has appeared in the *New York Times*, *New York* magazine, the *Village Voice*, *Harper's Bazaar*, and many other publications. She edited the popular, award-winning anthology *Goodbye to All That: Writers on Loving and Leaving New York*, is a columnist for The Rumpus, and teaches writing workshops through the nonprofit TMI Project and elsewhere.